SOCIO-PSYCHOLOGICAL DIMENSIONS OF WOMEN EDUCATION

SOCIO-PSYCHOLOGICAL DIMENSIONS OF WOMEN EDUCATION

By

Dr. S.S. MATHUR
and
Dr. (Mrs.) Anju Mathur

GYAN

Socio-Psychological
Dimensions of Women Education

Dr. S.S. Mathur
and
Dr. (Mrs.) Anju Mathur
ISBN : 978-81-212-0748-5

First Published 2001, reprint 2013 in India by
Gyan Publishing House
23, Main Ansari Road, Daryaganj,
New Delhi - 110002
Phones : 23282060, 23261060

Fax : (011) 23285914
E-mail: books@gyanbooks.com
website: gyanbooks.com

Printed at : Sagar Color Scan, New Delhi.

CONTENTS

PREFACE

All the civilized nations realize the importance of the women education. In India also serious efforts are made to provide education to all the girls of school-going age. Many agencies are establishing centres for the education of the adult women who have been deprived of education in their childhood. There is thus much quantitative expansion in the area of women education. Still the situation is far from satisfactory. The literacy percentage among Indian women is awfully low. This may be due to the low social status assigned to the Indian women by the conservative males. It may also be due to the psychological make up of the women themselves. The present book makes an effort to examine the socio-psychological dimensions of women education in India.

Since the ancient to the modern times, the Indian women has been enmeshed in a web of myth and reality. She was put at a high pedestal as a Devi, the goddess. On the other hand she was also branded as evil incarnate. Entangled in this web, her education suffered a lot. In the present book this aspect is probed and reality-oriented approaches towards her education are emphasized.

The book is the result of research studies conducted by the author and some of his students. Dr. (Mrs.) Anju Mathur has been associated with this work throughout the preparation and writing stage. Dr. (Mrs.) Usha Dhawari's research work has also been very helpful in formulating futuristic trends for women education. The author is deeply indebted to both of them.

The author expresses his heartfelt thanks to his wife Mrs. Urmila Mathur who gave him full cooperation during the period of his writing work. He also wishes to thank his sons Rajiv Mathur and Sanjay Mathur who helped him in the computerization of the manuscript. Thanks are also due to his daughters-in-law—Renu Mathur and Seema Mathur.

The publishers have been quite helpful and have offered very pertinent suggestions from time to time. The author expresses his gratitude to them. Lastly he wishes to acknowledge the contribution of those authors whose work have been referred to in the text of the book.

October 7, 2000 **S.S. Mathur**

INTRODUCTION

The woman has been the subject of study from the ancient to the modern times. Comments on the nature of women—their ambitions and aspirations, desires and wishes, birth and upbringing, relations with husband, paramour, children and other relatives have been the subject of discussion, comments, conversations and investigations throughout the history of mankind. The woman has been branded as a mysterious creature as well as a devoted mother and self-sacrificing wife during various periods of time through which the human civilization has evolved out from its primitive roots to an advanced scientific and technical culture.

The changing status and position of the woman in different periods and in different civilizations have very greatly influenced her upbringing and education. If during one period of time or in one civilization she was brought up as a prized possession of the parents, in some others she was completely neglected and was accepted only as a provider of sexual pleasure to man and as a producer of his offspring. As a provider of pleasure and producer of children, her education was completely neglected but whenever and wherever she was given high prestige in society, her education became the primary concern of the social order. Thus, the education of the woman has been completely limited to her sociological status and psychological make up. In the present book the focus is on the social-psychological dimensions of a women education in India.'

For better understanding of the socio-psychological dimensions of women education in India one may look into the background out of which the role, position and education of women have emerged from the past to the present. In the following pages the authors have presented a brief description of women's role, position and education in the religious and historical perspectives. The authors have confined their description mainly to the Indian women but have also focused attention on the women in the West in the context of their struggle for emancipation and empowerment in order to visualize its influence on the Indian womanhood.

Woman in Hindu Thought

Oronically, very little information is available about the civilization in pre-Aryan India. However, opinion of some archaeologists is that the non-Aryans had originated in India as early as around 2500 B.C. and were of mixed origin and diverse ethnic composition. Later, their intellectual bent of mind influenced the Aryan thought process. The law of karma, reincarnation, animal veneration, female or earth-mother goddesses, deity worship and male and female fertility symbols might have been imbibed by the Aryans from them.

It seems that to begin with the Aryans overwhelmed the non-Aryans, suppressed their religion and culture and imposed their own values. However, as time passed the Aryans became progressively Indianized, they absorbed the customs of the original inhabitants and modified their religion assimilating the existing culture. The Aryans' own religious and social customs were fused with theirs and Indianized by the native people. Thus, fusing together of incoming concepts and prevailing customs became the tradition of India and of Hinduism.

The Aryans produced vedic literature. The philosophies of Vedanta and Upanishads are their contributions.

Aryan family life was stable. The society was founded on the institutions of home and family. The women were assigned prestigious position in the social order. The Rig Vedic expression "the wife is the home"—shows how domestic life was woven around the woman.

The pre-vedic society was basically matriarchal. It worshipped a goddess of earth-mother type. The Aryan society was patriarchal but the worship of the goddess prevailed. Earlier the mother goddess was worshipped in the form of icons but the Aryans almost replaced the icons with matronly women, real mothers who were human and humane. The mother was given a high status in all the spheres of life.

There was attached great importance to the goddess Aditi who typified the motherhood. She was considered the ideal mother like Maat of the Egyptians and Themis of the Greeks. Her function has been described to tenderly look after the living beings.

Rig Vedic Aryans loved their wives and children. They had a desire for male child but the birth of a daughter as a potential mother was also accepted and welcomed. However, in Rig Veda no desire for a daughter is expressed, while in Atharva Veda the birth of a daughter is even deprecated. In Upanishads there are prescribed certain rituals to be performed by a man who wants a learned daughter to be born.

In the Rg Vedic period the son and daughter were not discriminated in their upbringing. The son was to take to the profession of the father, while the daughter was to inherit the glory and honour of her mother. The wife as mother was given the dignity and respect in the household. She was expected to perform duties which were both of celestial as well as terrestial in nature. She participated in all sacrifices instituted by her husband.

Education of Women According to Hindu Scriptures

Women were educated both in the spiritual as well as temporal subjects. They were given training in the religious lore, in the historical tradition and mythology. They were also given training in the fine arts as well as in the military science in certain cases. As a qualification for marriage, the education of a girl was considered as important as that of a boy.

The education of the women mainly centred round the acquisition of language and literature, the fine arts and the military science. The ancient literature records that there were scores of women, eligible to become *Rishis* and, composed very effective poetry. The name of Ghosa, the wife of the great seer Kaksivan can be mentioned. In Rg Veda she has been mentioned many a time. Two long hymns, 39 and 40 of the tenth *mandala* stand to her credit. Lopamundra is another lady *Rishi* who is credited with having composed a hymn jointly with her husband Agastya.

Music was a necessary equipment for women of the period. Songs were sung on all important occasions and functions. Dancing as an art was also learnt by the women. The women were also trained in self-defence. They knows how to use bow and arrow.

The paternal and maternal tie was very strong among the early Aryans. The father was respected as the earner and protector, the mother was loved for providing daily nourishment and maintaining the household. The daughter was caressed and fondled by her parents and brothers who gave her lavish presents at the time of her marriage. She was considered the breath and life of the family.

The women had liberty of movement. There was no *Parda*. Indo-Aryans recognized the truth embodied in the dictums, "Ignorance is weakness," "Knowledge is power".

Women in Upanishadic Texts

The member of Upanishads is estimated to be around fifty. In most of them, we do not find any reference to women. It is only in Chandogya and Brihadaranyaka Upanishads that we find that women were admitted into philosophical groups and were allowed to discuss the highest spiritual truths of life. They enjoyed a position at par with men. The men and women were considered as the 'two wheels of the same chariot.

From the account of this period we find that women were free from social constraints. Girls were free to choose their own husbands. They married only after attaining puberty. The women were even exalted to the position of goddess and given different celestial names like Prithvi, a vague personification of the earth, Usha, the goddess of the dawn, Ratri, the spirit of night etc.

The concept of Ardhanarishwara was propagated. The concept was that of a figure image of half Shiva and the other half as Parvati. This image signified the interdependence of men and women. It conveyed the message that separately men and women are incomplete. Only jointly they are complete. The figure image depicted the masculine and the feminine functions of the Supreme being.

It may be noted that in the Upanishadic texts woman was no eulogized as a person in herself but first and foremost her role as wife and mother was given high status and value. The women were idealized and glorified as mothers. The girl as a potential perpetuator of a family line was valued as much as a son.

Since Rg Vedic age education of women was given much importance. There is evidence that the discipline of brahamacharya was also required to be observed by the girl. The stage of brahamacharya in all probability may be the period of studentship of the girl preceding her married life. The girls were taught that marriage was not for lust, but for perfect domestic life and for producing illustrious progeny. They were given training in the art of house keeping and house management. Their education was to prepare them to conduct themselves properly in the married life. They learnt the art of some handicrafts, the elements of hygiene, physiology and nutrition.

The pattern of education in the Upanishadic period became more philosophical in nature. The men and women shifted their attention from Vedic ritualism to more intricate problems of life. The women engaged themselves freely in debates .nd philosophical symposia.

Education helped the women to become more balanced and lead a regulated good life. It was directed towards the development of their natural virtues and latent capabilities and aimed at all round development of their character and personality. Eminent women scholars of this period like Sulabha, Vadya, Maitreyi and Gargi made significant contributions to the advancement of knowledge.

Manu's Views about Women

A description of status, position and education of the women of ancient India is incomplete without the mention of Manu's views. *Manusmrithi* (about 200 B.C.) prescribes duties and obligations of a woman. For Manu, woman is a perpetual minor and has to lead whole of her life under the guardianship of either the father, the husband or the son.

Manu prescribes that the wife must always worship her husband as God even if he is debauch, immoral and lacks good qualities. It is the bounden duty of the wife to obey and follow the dictates of her husband. The woman's salvation lies only in the devoted service to her husband. He refers to her duties in the following words:

> "She must always be cheerful, clever in the management of her household affairs, careful in cleaning her utensils, and economical in expenditure"[1]

Manu favoured only the domestic and religious education for women. He also favoured the giving of training in music and dance to the woman in order that she may be able to please her man.

Education of the Women in the Epic Period

The society in the Epic period was completely patriarchal and patrilineal, so the husband was considered the senior partner in the home. But the wife was also given the dignity in the household because of her vocation of motherhood. Her virtues were recognized. Her abilities in the maintenance of the household were appreciated. She was considered to be a true friend of man given by God. She was man's half, his religious partner, giver of joy and sons.

The epics *Ramayana* and *Mahabharata* contain the

description of women who presented ideal conduct and models for the womenhood to be adopted by the lesser mortals. But these models also have ingrained in themselves the subordination of the women. Thus the epics trace the story of the rise and fall of the status of women in Hindu society. Mentioned below are a few highly revered and illustrious ladies who form the central theme of these epics.

Sita

The foremost among all the ladies mentioned in epics is Devi Sita. Sita is a paragon of virtue. She is an ideal wife who serves her husband with complete devotion, who is an 'embodiment of the spiritual sublimity of feminine character.' She suffers great hardships but remains unperturbed by them. Her only wish is to serve her husband with all her capabilities. She has to suffer the ordeal of fire but at no occasion she expresses any doubt in her loyalty, fidelity, devotion, love and sacrifice for the well being of her husband. She is learned. She can quote moral tales and smrities. She had religious education.

No doubt the ideal of Sita has inspired Indian women for ages. But in the modern times some are raising doubts about the complete subordination to the husband eulogised in the character of Sita. For educationists, it is a dilemma. Should the women education be directed towards the flowering of the women as devoted as Sita to her husband or teach them for independent outlook. For a proper answer all the aspcts of Sita's personality as portrayed in the epic have to be carefully examined. One thing stands out that is Sita had her own will and determination and even when she had to undergo torture her determination did not waver.

Draupadi

She was one of the strong-willed women of the Epic period. She possessed not only physical charm but also a brilliant mind. She was exposed to the brutalities of men when she was forced to discard her clothes before the men of the Kauravas court. But she did not lose the balance of her mind and reasoning power. The arguments presented by her in the Kaurava court were so perfect that nobody except Vidura and Vikarna possessed the courage to reply to her question. In the midst of her humiliation, she still showed good manners and saluted those Kuru elders who did not dare to check the evil. She was deeply learned and had comprehensive knowledge of old traditions, history and the Puranas. She did not hesitate in condemning her husbands when they failed in the performance of their duties. She did not tolerate her insult and inspired even a peace loving man like Yudhistira to war.

Draupadi presents to us an ideal of womanhood who was learned, iron willed, revengeful, intolerant towards undignified behaviour, loving and affectionate and also forgiving. She was a perfect wife, wise counsellor and dear companion to her husbands.

Other Learned Ladies of Epic Period

Among the other learned ladies of the Epic period we may name Gandhari, Kunti, Kaushalya, Sumitra, Kaikeyi, Gautami, Sulabha, Mandodri, Trigata and many others.

Gandhari was the noblest of mothers. She had understanding, judgment, intellect and good sense. She remained attached to the cause of justice and righteousness even when her sons were on the verge of being annihilated and their empire destroyed. She had a high sense of justice, possessed great intellectual qualities and depicted in her conduct both human virtues and frailties. She was jealous of Kunti's motherhood and had a longing for a daughter and son-in-law in order to attain Heaven. She spent her life in penance, self denial and righteousness. But she had weaknesses which make her character real and thus presents ideals which are attainable by ordinary human beings.

Kunti was an ideal wife and mother. She was also of strong will. She taught her sons to die gloriously in war than live in infamy. She was unwed mother of Karna whom she threw in the river. But her love for her son was irresistible, sublime and pure. Kunti presents an ideal of womanhood which is unflinching in love, righteousness yet not so bold as to face the hostile society for her begetting a son out of wedlock.

The three queens of king Dashratha-Kaushalya, Sumitra and Kaikeyi were well-versed in household affairs but were also involved in the state craft. They had many virtues but also sufferred from human frailties. Kaushalya was the ordinary human being but served her husband as a slave, friend, sister, wife, and mother. Sumitra was calm, steady and balanced. For her the path of duty and righteousness was more important than any material possession. Kaikeyi was dominating, bold and resourceful. Her life shows that she was over-ambitious and wished to control the kingdom through her husband and later through her son. She is by and large portrayed as a negative character.

There are many other women whose lives and exploits are presented as the ideals of Hindu womanhood. These ladies were highly cultured and were prepared to sacrifice personal good for the social good. The education of the Indian women, particularly the Hindu women has been very greatly influenced by the ideals propagated through the study of their lives and exhortations. However, in the modern times some questions are being asked about the ideals so propagated. In the various chapters of this book we will examine these doubts and try to arrive at some conclusions regarding their validity in the twenty-first century.

The Education of Women in Buddhist Thought

Buddha inculcated in his followers a reverence for learning. He conveyed the Dharma or Truth to his first disciples at his teaching sessions at Varanasi. These disciples became the first members of the Sangha. Among his first upasikas or followers there were two women. Initially he was reluctant to incorporate women into the Sangha and this attitude resulted in the subsequent neglect of female education by his followers.

Buddha believed that seven factors lead to wisdom:

inner mindfulness, searching of the norms, energy, zest, serenity, concentration, and mental balance. These thoughts were instilled in the young Buddhist males but were ignored in the case of sisters of the Sangha. As indicated above Buddha initially was averse to the admission of women into his Sangha system but later on agreed to the formation of the order of the nuns. These nuns were imparted religious and spiritual education. A life of celibacy, austerity and strict mental discipline was expected of them. The education for the women was also introduced at the later stage in order to help them to acquire the knowledge that would enable them to lead a fuller life. But the end of Buddhist era in India also resulted in the end of female education for many generations.

Women Education in Jainism

In Jainism, there was given great importance to self-denial, restrains of passion and a life of renunciation. A life of restraint and devoid of passion was expected from men and women. The women were also admitted into monasteries and given full facilities to get the best possible education. The Jaina system of education had depth, was universal in nature and applicable to all alike, irrespective of caste, creed or sex.

The spiritually trained Jaina women attained a high degree of academic education and involved themselves in preaching their faith of universal love and brotherhood. They dedicated themselves to social service.

Jainism was divided into two main sects-Digambaras and Shwetambaras. The Digambaras were of the opinion that women were incapable of attaining salvation and so did not admit them into their order. The Shwetambaras, on the other hand, made no distinction between the sexes and freely admitted aspirants of both the sexes into their order.

Theoretically, Jaina believed that man and women both had the right to attain perfection or perfect liberation of the highest order. But in practice Jaina felt that there were very few women who had the strength of mind and body to endure the hard life of an ascetic. The women were considered weak and so unfit to undertake a course of self-mortification and self-effacement. Thus in the spiritual order women had secondary position.

Women Education in Sikh Thought

Sikhism considers woman as worthy of respect as man's helpmate and a partner in his domestic life. Women are not looked upon as evil or perpetuator of sin, nor simply the objects of men's pleasure. A woman's roles as mother, wife, sister and daughter are praised and the qualities which the women are expected to develop are love, obedience, contentment and sweet temper.

Sikhism advocated equality among all the human beings. The social equality of the women is ungrudgingly recognized. The militant brotherhood of the Sikhs, the Khalsa, founded by Guru Gobind Singh in the seventeenth century was open to both sexes and all classes. The women were initiated into the Khalsa by taking the name of Kaur and were expected to perform the same duties as men.

Since in Sikhism the equality of sexes was recognized, very few restrictions were put on women education.

Women in Christianity

In Christianity, women are considered as the harbringer of evil. No doubt Catholics give a high respectful place to Virgin Marry but both Protestants and Catholics feel that the women brought the evil to the earth. The fall of Adam is attributed to the evil design of Eve. Hence the pious and saintly Christians like St. Bernard, St. Antony, St. Bonaventure, St. Geogroy the great, all cursed women. The woman was described by them as 'the organ of the devil', 'a scorpion ever ready to sting', 'the poison of an asp', 'the malice of the dragon' and 'the instrument which the devil uses to get possession of our souls'.

The position of the woman in the Jewish faith was very low but in Christianity it was further lowered. They charge her with the crime of disobeying God, causing the fall of Adam and her guilt being transmitted to the whole mankind so that every child is born in sin. Since God had to send Jesus to be sacrificed because of the first crime of the woman, so she is considered responsible for the crucification of Jesus. The Christian saints and priests considered women to be unclean and so gave much importance to a life of celibacy. It is because of this attitude that the Christian women were denied those rights and privileges which Christian men enjoyed. It is only in twentieth century that the movements of women liberation have resulted in their recognition as equals to men. The women had to wage a severe and persistent battle to achieve those rights which should have been their on the basis of their recognition as a part of humanity.

It is true that women have now been given rights. But they obtained these by their own struggle and by the slackening of the hold of priests over western societies and laws.

Education, historically, was the sole privilege of the rich and the priestly class. The priests dominated the transmission of knowledge throughout Christiandom. They controlled the access to institutions of learning. In all the Christian countries education was the monopoly of the religious orders. The governing priests did not consider the education of women essential. They were of the view that women were incapable of absorbing the same amount of education or the same in-depth knowledge as men. Besides this they thought that women's minds were weaker than men's and did not require that intellectual exercise which the men needed. They had spread the myth that women should be restrained from speaking in church and from getting education.

The Christian priests' disregard for women education was rooted in their belief in women's inferiority. This disregard was further reinforced by the fear of female emancipation. They were afraid that free education may lead to the deployment of women's full potential.

This in their view was going to upset the natural order between men and women and God and women and the church. They emphatically pointed out that the women are modest, obedient and docile and as such do not require as thorough education as men do.

Later the missionaries started giving education to women but they segregated boys and girls and prescribed different courses of study to the two sexes. The boys were taught useful subjects in the vocational, mechanical and scientific spheres. The girls were taught domesticity, cookery, knitting etc. The idea was that boys should be prepared for life outside home and the girls for life inside the home.

As we have already pointed out that the situation has very much changed now in almost all the Christian countries but still the stigma attached of being the women has not been completely wiped out. And whatever women have achieved in raising their status and position and in attaining prestige has been the fruits of their own struggle for emancipation and empowerment.

Women in Islamic Traditions

In Islam straight forward directions regarding the status and the position of the women have been laid down. It is the only religion in which the universal laws for all the walks of human life are laid down including that for women. There are directions regarding social and political rights of women. There are laws regarding their claims to property and their privileges for the custody of children and their religious duties.

Islam gives equality to women in relation to men in many respects. It makes a case for the dignity of women. In holy Quran it is mentioned that "women are the twin halves of men". "The world and all things in it are valuable but the most valuable thing in the world is a virtuous wife", "God enjoins upon you to treat women well for they are your mothers, daughters and aunts"[2].

There are also many aspects which present seeds of discrimination between men and women. Islam gives rights of inheritance of property to women as a daughter, a wife, a mother, a sister and in some cases even to more distantly related. But when a man has a son and a daughter both, the share of the daughter is half that of the son.

The inequality between men and women is also evident in Islam when we find that women are put in seclusion in Islam. They are put behind *parda* and debarred from any male company besides their immediate and near relations. Other areas of discrimination are man's right of divorce, the right of men to practice polygamy, have four wives at a time and similar other provisions like "the testimonies of two women are equal to one man". Parda system isolated women from the outer world and confined them to the four walls of their house.

In the holy Quoran the women are exhorted to be modest, chaste, lead a life of decorum and decency which was interpreted by the religious leaders in terms of putting the women in Parda, put a veil or burkah on their bodies. This resulted in losing their right to participate in communal activities. Thus Islam differentiated between the man's world and the woman's world.

In early Islam, female education was highly restricted. Only in the families in which the father was educated, the girls learnt to recite the verses of Quoran. But her learning was totally dependent on the approval of the father.

In the medieval period women education was by and large ignored. The women were excluded from public gatherings or in any intellectual deliberations. The result was that most of the women remained illiterate and unlettered. Some female had access to tutors and libraries but they were not engaged by men-folk in any intellectual discussion. Hence they could learn through their own individual efforts. By and large women remained in status as inferior, unequal, submissive and ignorant beings. Females were denied access to learning. They were also excluded from the mosques where most of the education occurred. They could not attend the Kuttabs and the Madrasah.

Some of the women who were fortunate to receive education usually came from affluent, prestigious families that could afford to hire private tutors and successfully face the criticism of the community for educating their females.

It is worth noticing that despite Islam giving equality to sexes and permitting men and women to acquire success, education and honour and inspite of it giving equal religious and spiritual rights the Islamic clergy interpreted it in terms of equality in their own natural sphere of being men and women. They propagated that the roles of men and women are different and so their education has to be isolated from each other. While man needs education woman has to stay at home and involve herself in house keeping for which the training in the house craft is only needed, which can be provided in the home itself.

Status of the Indian Women at Various Periods of Her History

Above we have described to role, status and education of Indian women as determined by the religious order to which they belonged. Let us now look into the status etc. of the Indian women in historical perspective.

Status of the Indian Women During Vedic Period

We have already emphasized that from the very beginning of the history of civilization society has been male dominated and the status and the position of the woman depended on how man conceived her in his relationship with her. In India the Rg Vedic society was founded on the home and family and so assigned a place of importance to her. The Rg Vedic sages wove the domestic life on the sentiments centred round the women. The women of the Vedic period participated in the religious, philosophical and social activities and made contributions to the Vedic and Brahmanic literature. The learned lady was held in high esteem.

In the Epic age the woman was considered to be a true friend of man. She was regarded as man's half, his religious partner, giver of joy and sons. Through her man was able to attain immortality. Sita, Savitri, Damyanti, Draupadi born in royal families and in luxury followed their husbands to the wilderness of the forests and endured a life of much hardships along with them. They embody in themselves extreme love, devotion and selfless service to their spouses. They served without expectations of any return from them. Women of this period were also ideal mothers and true teachers of their offspring.

There is evidence that the Muslim invasion brought about the deterioration of women's position. Restrictions on her rights and freedom were imposed. Muslims adherence to Polygamy and *Parda* also influenced the Hindus. Restrictions of the rights and privileges of the women were imposed. The women were considered inferior to men and so began to be ill-treated. The women, both among Hindus and Muslims were confined to their homes and their duties, rights or obligations all were interpreted in terms of devoted wife and sacrificing mother.

The position of the medieval Muslim woman, according to Muslim law was somewhat better than that of contemporary Hindu woman. But in practice it was similar or in many instances inferior than Hindu woman because of the rigidity of the *Parda* system and the denial of education to Muslim women.

There is no authentic account of the prevalence of education among Muslim women of classes and masses. However, it seems that the majority of Muslim women were illiterate and those few who were educated learnt through oral and non-formal instructions. There were ladies of the noble families who had the privilege of learning the religious texts and various arts and crafts but those they learnt by their own persistence and in their own homes. History reveals that there were highly learned and accomplished Muslim ladies like Razia Sultan, Chand Bibi, Nur Jahan, Jahanara etc. These ladies could learn and attain dominance by sheer strength of their personality. Thus we may conclude that during Muslim period while the women from royal families enjoyed much respect and freedom and were interested in learning, the women of lower and middle strata of society were largely ignorant and illiterate.

Status and Position of Women in British India

At the advent of the British Empire the status and the position of the Indian women were very low. From the ideological point of view women was considered a complete inferior species. She was inferior to male having no personality, no significance. From the social point of view she was kept in a state of utter subjection, denied any right, suppressed and oppressed.

The customs of polygamy, the parda, the denial of woman's rights over property, child marriage, sati pratha and denial of remarriage to widows—all these practices in this period resulted in the development of a very weak personality of the woman. She was not only considered an inferior by the male members of the society but she in herself became rooted to the idea that she was weak, helpless, subordinate and inferior—a non entity, a slave. Hence women themselves became great perpetuators of tyranny on the women over whom they could exercise their sadism. So dowry demands, forcing of the widows to burn or to lead a life of misery and toil, a dominant mother-in-law and subservient daughter-in-law, all such act were initiated, perpetuated and committed by the women or in connivance with the women.

The British influence was in the positive direction. The close contacts with western cultural tradition, literature and education affected very deeply the minds of the Indian leaders. The result of it was the social movements for reforms in those evils which were prevalent in the society. The reformist movements started in the 19th century. The leaders and the social reformers who were in the forefront of the struggle for women emancipation were Raja Ram Mohan Roy, Ishwar Chandra Vidhyasagar, Swami Dayanand Saraswati, Swami Vivekanand, Mahatma Gandhi, Jawahar Lal Nehru and many others.

To Raja Ram Mohan Roy goes the credit of laying the foundations of all the principle reformist movements which subsequently became instruments for modernization of the country. He devoted whole of his life for raising the status and position of the women in India. He propagated his own democratic, rational and human conception of womanhood.

It is said that while Raja saved the widow from self-immolation or becoming Sati on the funeral pyre of her husband, Ishwar Chandra Vidyasagar released her from a living death, by helping to legalize the Widow Remarriage. He wrote a book on widow remarriage which was published in 1853. It was through his efforts that the widow remarriage Act of 1856 was passed which permitted the legitimacy of the issues born of such marriages. He also gave much importance to the education of the girls which was considered essential for the development of their personality. Swami Dayanand Saraswati felt that the woman's status must be raised. He sought to create equal status for the women in the field of Sacred Thread Ceremony. He considered that education must aim at making women capable of performing her duties in home as well as outside the home. He founded Arya Samaj in 1875 at Bombay. It started Gurukuls for widows, rescue homes for destitutes etc.

Another social reformer was Swami Vivekanand. He was greatly pained at miserable condition of women in India. He, therefore, recommended that women should be supported and educated as men. He said, "It is only in the hands of educated and pious mothers the great men are born. The ideal woman in India is that mother, the mother first and the mother last." He suggested that the women should be made ambitious through a sound system of education. For him the ideal of womanhood was not only Sita or Savitri but that of an ideal mother. He said "Motherhood is the beginning. Motherhood is the end of Indian womanhood."

Mahatma Gandhi considered that if husband is a God, the wife is a Goddess. Wife is not a slave but a friend and companian with equal rights. Gandhi held the view that women have a right to education. But he was of this view that men and women are not identical but complementary to one another. Education for them should be such that it make both of them capable of performing their duties. Gandhiji's efforts led to the elevation of the woman's status and involved her in the struggle for social progress and political independence. The women were able to develop their latent powers. Women like Sarojini Naidu, Kasturba Gandhi, Kamla Nehru, Aruna Asaf Ali participated in the social and political arena with all their might and potentials. Indeed India witnessed the rise of many great women.

India gained freedom in 1947. Her Constitution was adopted on 26th January, 1950. The constitution gave full and equal rights to women as compared to men. Thereafter we are witnessing a strong, persistent and unrelenting struggle for the emancipation, empowerment and dignity led by women activists, enlightened political leaders, educationist and social reformers.

Status and Position of the Women in the Western Countries

The western countries being mostly Christianity dominated gave the status and the position to the women as dictated by their religion. Hence in most of them till quite recently women were given a very low status in comparison to men. The Christians considered the women as temptations of the world of flesh and of the devil. The fathers of the church believed in the myth that Eve led Adam into sin.

Earlier, before the advent of Christianity, the women of Greece enjoyed much better status and position than later Christian women. Plato, the Greek philosopher made no distinction of the sexes in his ideal 'Republic'. He, no doubt, admits that women are generally inferior to men but in his view they have similar, if lower, capacities and power. He emphasized that there is no occupation or art for which they may not be fitted by nature and education. He, therefore, wants them to share in government and war as well as in the various mechanical trades. Still the Greek opinion was that women are best suited for household chores. Aristotle had unshakable faith in the value of household and the family and considered man as its natural ruler.

> The Romans held women in greatest honour as the words of Cato the Censor show: "All men, rule over women, we Romans rule over all men, and our wives rule over us."[3]

In law, however, the women had an inferior status in that they did not have freedom. They were always put under the control of some male member of the family. Before marriage she was entirely under the control of father, on her marriage she passed into a similar position towards her husband, and if she remained unmarried, she was under the control of her nearest male relative. In spite of this legal position, the position of the women in their family was an honoured one. Roman girls did not, as a rule, go to school. They were taught all that they were to know of book learning at home by their mothers.

When Christianity came a new set of virtues began to be propagated in place of the vices which had engulfed the later Roman social order. It is to be noted that the Roman society, in the beginning of the Christian era, had become a completely debunked society in which ethical and moral values were completely eroded. Christianity combined and harmonized an ideal of personal morality, sincerity, honesty, chastity, love, loyalty, kindness and unselfishness. Womanhood was elevated and given a new dignity. Before the establishment of Christianity, divorce became frequent, infanticide, child exposure, cruel and bloody gladiatorial shows, licentiousness in private life were the evils which had deformed the society. Christianity fought against these evils and created a better and just order. Women, even though remained under the subjection of male members, yet were given an honoured place in home.

In the early middle ages, from the sixth to the tenth centuries, the creeds and dogmas established by the church were accepted without any doubts or questions. But after tenth century, particularly, during the eleventh and twelfth centuries, Christian scholars started questioning the dogmas spread by the church. They adopted logical methods of discussion and analysed the various beliefs and faiths on the anvil of rationality. This period is, therefore, known as the period of Scholasticism. "The aim of Scholasticism was to support the doctrines of the church by rational argument, to show essential harmony between reason and faith." The thirteenth century was the Golden Age of Scholasticism. In this age, Scholasticism projected two high peaks. One was that of the doctrine of St. Thomas, who along with Albert built Aristotelianism into a Christian system of thought. The other was that of St. Bonaventure. At this peak, the Augustinian thought of the middle ages reached its highest development. St. Thomas and St. Bonaventure were two sages who led to the construction of Schólastic synthesis of the middle ages.

We find in general in the doctrines of the church of the middle ages that women was represented as the source of all evils in the world. St. Franciscan Bonaventure wrote.

> "Women is an embarrassment to man, a beast in his quarters, a continual worry, a never ending trouble, a daily annoyance, the destruction of the householo, a hinderance to solitude, the undoing of a virtuous man, an oppressive burden, an insatiable bee, man's property and possession."[4]

The view of St. Thomas Aquinas (1225-1274) about women were almost similar in that he also considered women inferior to men. He might be greatly influenced by the opinion of the age. In his opinion man represents in himself perfection, while woman stands for the imperfect. He also depreciates the functions of the woman. Woman is dependent on man for procreation and for guidance throughout her life whereas man needs woman only for procreation. Man is thus master and woman a mere helper. The woman h s weaker body, the smaller growth and weaker intellect and lesser will-power.

During Scholastic period it was not compulsory for girls to go to the school. To them domestic education was given in their homes. The University rules did not allow the admission of women in the Universities.

The Protestant Revolt

Martin Luther (1483-1546) criticised and protested against certain practices of the established church of his times. He tried to combine the best ideals of the past with religious morality and a new idealistic approach to Christian religion developed in Protestantism. The Protestants advocated an honourable and equal status for women like men. According to them the man is the embodiment of the strength, power and greatness while woman is the embodiment of the smooth, gentle, softness and beauty. Man and woman are complement of each other. Their relationship is not that of a master and a slave. The Protestant reformers also advocated universal, compulsory and free education for all classes and for both men and women.

Renaissance Humanism

The Protestant revolt was accompanied and followed by the humanists who initiated the period known as Renaissance. These humanist rejoiced the theological dialectic of Scholasticism. In this period the emphasis was laid on the popular and universal education for both men and women. The woman was now not given an inferior status but was recognized as an active partner of man in bringing progress and prosperity to the society. Comenius demanded education for all children, rich and poor, boys and girls, in all cities and towns, villages and hamlets. John Locke and Hobbes recognized that familial authority belonged to the mother as well as to the father.

The Protestant revolt did not put equal influence in all the countries of Europe. However, in France, the State, church and the government achieved a considerable degree of independence from Rome. At this time Jean Jacques Rousseau introduced the philosophy of Naturalism in education. However, his philosophy of education did not follow the principle of equality in the education of men and women. For him the procreative role of woman make her unlike man. Functionally the women are determined by their reproductive role. He also implied in his attitude towards women education that they are the source of evil. Modesty is the only virtue of a woman and man has the absolute right over his wife.

He gave a long list of women characteristics like shame, stupidity, weakness and ignorance. He was of the view that intellectual pursuits are not for the women. Nature intended women for domestic functions mainly. For him the duty of the woman was only to please man. So woman has to learn singing, dancing, embroidery and designing. She may receive an early education in morals and religion so that she can provide a good home for her family.

The psychological developmentalists like Pestalozzi, Herbart and Froebal were of different view that the woman is neither physically weak nor morally inferior to man. She is the active sharer of sorrows and sufferings of life with man. Pestalozzi believed that it was possible to improve the status and position of woman only through education. Herbart emphasized that the aim of the education of the woman should be to analyse her interests, to discover which are best for her and for society and apply these interests in the various situations in life. His emphasis was that education of woman should develop the will to be good and the desire to make sould moral choices resulting in a high degree of personal character and social morality. According to Froebel, "Education must be controlled development by which both man and woman come into realization of the life of the all encompassing, unity of which both of them are a part, a development by which their lives broaden until it has related itself to nature, until it enters sympathetically into all the activities of the society, until it enters into the achievements of the race and the aspirations of humanity". Thus it may be concluded that the developmentalists consider woman having equal position like that of man. They are the active members of the society who help to make better home and society.

Jeremy Bentham was a covert feminist. He wanted to

put untapped brains and energies of women to use. He believed that the sensibility of women is greater than men. The woman is more fit for a family life and man for outside life. But Bentham did not want to exclude women altogether from public life.

James Stuart Mill emphasized that the emancipation of women has a two way effect: "they themselves be happy, they will add to the happiness of society". Hence he laid stress on the women education as the surest way to cultivate them and to free them from the bonds of domesticity by opening up careers for them. Mill criticized the theory of inner inferiority of women as supported by Aristotle and Rouseau. But Mill did not question the traditional family system and its demands on women.

Socialist Thinkers

Among the socialists Marx and Engels are predominant. They were the forerunners of the doctrine of communism. According to this doctrine they preached that through the institution of family, the children became private heirs which meant the women's reproductive labour like their productive work underwent a transformation from social to private. And this led to the subordination of women in terms of the emergence of the private property.

Woman's Emergence from the Inferior Status and Position

The description given above about the status, position and education of the women both in India and western countries indicate that women, by and large, were given much inferior status and position in most of the periods of history and by most of the thinkers with a few exceptions. The great philosophers like Plato, Aristotle, St. Thomas Aquinas, Rousseau and others talked much of equality and goodness of mankind but did not acknowledge the same goodness and equality to women. John Stuart Mill may be taken as an exception. The social theorists considered that institution of private property was the root cause of relegating women to a secondary position.

The situation so far presented started to change in the later part of the nineteenth century and the beginning of twentieth century. The women education began to spread. The Industrial Revolution, American Independence and the world wars awakened the western women. Further the political upheavals and revolutions in USSR, France, India and China made the women aware of their enslavement by the male members of the society. The women began to demand equal rights with men.

The Industrial Revolution in Europe ushered a new era in the emergence of women from their homes to engage various other vocations. It inspired the women's movement for bringing change in their status and position. The First World War brought dramatic alteration in the image of woman. At the end of it the opportunities of women's employment increased many-fold.. The women also asserted in their freedom of dress and in smoking and drinking in public.

The Second World War brought almost four million new women workers. There was an upsurge in the demand of women's equal rights with men. The women education spread rapidly. The women now entered in all types of professions along with the right to speak in public, to vote for and hold office. There was a revolt against the double standards of morality and against puritanism. As twentieth century advanced the women adopted swim suits, short skirts, started taking part in sports, driving cars etc. The women got greater leisure by the introduction of mechanized kitchens. By the middle of the twentieth century women's liberation. Movements became more vigorous and involved more and more women's organizations, in Europe in general and in America in particular. The women now presented the cult of new feminism. It demanded full social equality for women. The women fought for more independence and discarded the traditional triangular roles for themselves-that of children, kitchen and the church. The women's organizations rejected the 'Barbi-doll' stereotypical model of woman. The middle class educated women were in the forefront of the struggle for women's rights and for presenting a new image of feminism. They protested against a passive, conforming, dependent female stereotyped roles and a future which tie them down to the home and family.

The women's movements have achieved much. Still, even in the west the women have not yet attained that position and status which they consider is equivalent to men. They are still fighting for equal pay, status, position and security like that of men. They have become intolerant to any discrimination in their service conditions because of their sex. The battle is going on.

Indian Women and the Struggle for their Emancipation

We have traced very briefly the history of women movements for empowerment, equality and recognition as worthy members of the society in the west. Let us now peep into the situation as it exists with respect to Indian women.

The Indian women have fallen from the high position and status held by them in Vedic times to a very degrading position in the medieval period and in the earlier decades of the modern period. It was for the enlightened Indians educated in the western tradition and culture that brought a change in the outlook of the Indian males and females regarding their mutual relationship. In Indian situation the movement for female emancipation was led in the beginning by the male members of the society. These Indian males who fought for a higher status and the position of women were those who were impressed by the regards and considerations which western women enjoyed but they made the case of women emancipation on the basis of the reinterpretation of Indian religious texts and exposing the gimmicks of the half literate clergy which advocated sati system and approved the ill treatment of widows, parda system, confining of the women to homes, child marriages and calling any women as *Kulta* or corrupt if she deviated slightly from the norms of conduct laid by them for women. For the ill-treatment of women they were drawing support from a perverted interpretation of the religious texts and religious precepts. The enlightened Indians exposed their misinterpretation and based their argument for women liberation on their own very well studied and expressed interpretation.

The movement for women emancipation was also undertaken by enlightened women like Pandita Rama Bai and others. They set the trend which was followed by hundreds of women. The freedom movement launched by Gandhiji drew women into the central field of struggle. Women fought for the freedom of the country as well as for their own emancipation. According to *Manu Smriti* Hindu women were given a right to stridhan properties but not to the joint family property on which she had only the right to maintenance. She was given an inferior position in the law of adoption. The status of the woman was determined according to the nature of relationship she had with a man. She was a "Sarvainini" as a wanton woman, "Veshya" as a prostitute, "Kishkashini" as a woman discarded by her paramour or a "Dasi" as a woman kept exclusively by the man.[5]

According to Justice Bhandare "It was only later that during the time of Vijanesvera that the archaic smriti law was freed from religious fetters and changed for the benefit of women".[6] But it took a long time and centuries of oppression that women got some legal rights over their property. It was only in 1937 that the concept of widow's estate was developed in respect of property inherited by her from her husband.[7]

The freedom struggle created an urge in the Indian male and female to ameliorate the condition of the down trodden and neglected sections of the society. The women, Scheduled Castes and Scheduled Tribes were some such sections. Hence when the constitution for an independent India was drawn, the emphasis was put on the development of an egalitarian society. For the elimination of discriminatory and derogatory practices against women Articles 14, 15(3), 16, 39(e) and 51 were introduced. These guarantee equality and special protection for women.

The Article 14 provided for equality of all before the

law. Article 15 emphasized that the "State shall not discriminate against any citizen on grounds only of religion, race, caste, sex, place of birth or any of them." Article 15 (3) stated that "Nothing in this article shall prevent the state from making any special provision for women and children." Article 16 mentioned that (1) there shall be equality of opportunity for all citizens in matters relating to employment or appointment to any office under the State. (2) No citizen shall, on grounds only of religion, race, caste, sex, descent, place of birth, residence or any of them be ineligible for, or discriminated against in respect of any employment or office under the State.

Article 39 States

"The State shall, in particular, direct its policy towards securing

(1) that the citizens, men and women equally, have the right to an adequate means of livelihood.

(2) that there is equal pay for equal work for both men and women.

(3) that the health and strength of workers, men and women and the tender age of children are not abused and that the citizens are not forced by economic necessity to enter avocations unsuited to their age or strength."

Article 51 A States

"It shall be the duty of every citizen of India to promote harmony and the spirit of common brotherhood amongst all the people of India transcending linguistic, logistic and regional or sectional diversities, to renounce practices derogatory to the dignity of women."

When the Universal Declaration of Human Rights was adopted on 10th December, 1948 its Article 1 provided that "all human beings are born free and equal in dignity and rights". Article 2 provided for equality of sexes. It states that "everyone is entitled to all the rights and freedoms without distinction of sex."

The International covenant on Civil and Political Rights, 1966 urges every covenant State to respect and ensure to all individuals within its territory the rights recognized by that covenant without distinction of sex. Article 3 of this documents emphasize that covenant States should undertake to ensure equal rights of men and women. In 1979 the convention on the Elimination of All Forms of Discrimination Against Women reiterated "that discrimination against women violates the principles of equality of rights and respect for women's dignity and is an obstacle to the participation of women on equal terms with men in the political, social, economic and cultural life of their countries, hampers the growth of prosperity of society and the family and makes more difficult the full development of the potentialities of women in the service of their countries and of humanity and urges that change in the traditional role of women as well as role of women in society and in the family is needed to achieve full equality between men and women".[9]

Justice Bhandare writes "In spite of the enshrinement of these provisions, equality between men and women continue to be an elusive goal, not only in our country but all over the world. A wide gap exists between the ideal and the practical in our country, partly due to historical reasons. However, the main reason why such discrimination continues in our country is the attitude of inferiority—nay bondage—towards women and an atmosphere in which women are deprived of all basic freedoms, starting with that of education, and are thereby exposed to easy exploitation".[10]

This book have concentrates on the women education and its impact on male-female discrimination and on the female psyche. In almost all the chapters, the book trief to highlight the importance of education to the girl child as well as to the grown up woman.

Justice Bhandare raises some questions regarding disparity between man and woman and says that several of those questions do not have an adequate and satisfactory answer. An attempt is made to seek answers to these and similar questions by focussing our attention on the triad of sociological, psychological and educational aspects of female development in our country. The questions raised by Justice Bhandare are:

(a) How is it that in public life—professions, business and services—women are not adequately represented?

(b) How is it that women put in longer hours of work compared to men and yet do not enjoy equal status or opportunities?

(c) Why is it that property owned by women constitutes a very small fraction of the property owned by men?

(d) Why is it that maternity is not recognized as an essential social function?

(e) Why is the rate of suicide so high among women?

(f) Why is it that fairness vanishes when it comes to giving a fair deal to the 'fair' sex.[11]

Movements for the Emancipation of Indian Women

The struggle for the emancipation of western women had its impact on the emancipation movements in India. But in India the feminist movement did not take the aggressive and militant form which it took in some European countries. In India the feminist movements were not vehemently or violently opposed by the male members, or clergy or politicians. Rather they were supported by enlightened political and religious thinkers. The agitations for female liberation in India began in the later part of the nineteenth century and were carried on with zeal till the Constitution of India in 1950 gave them equality in terms of their lawfull existence. Those agitations were largely spear-headed by women reformists and male thinkers who had the best of western education. These movements emphasized on the need of the small middle class educated and privileged women. The real breakthrough in the recognition of male-female equalities was made only when the Constitution of the Indian Republic was adapted in 1950.

Before that in 1949 the University Education Commission which was set up under the Chairmanship of Dr. S. Radhakrishnan has observed:

> "There cannot be educated people without educated women. If general education had to be limited to men or to women, the opportunity should be given to women, for then it would more surely be passed on to the next generation".[12]

The secondary education commission (1952-53) emphasized that

"Every type of education open to men should also be open to women". Thus this commission did not make any distinction between the education of men and women and so era of equality of educational opportunities to women began.

The Report of the National Committee on Women's Education (1958-59) made a strong case for the education of women. Its important recommendation was:

> "The education of women should be regarded as a major and a special problem in education for a good many years to come and a bold and determined effort should be made to face its difficulties and magnitude and to close the existing gap between the education of men and women in as short a time as possible".[14]

As has been specified earlier the movements for women emancipation in India were largely initiated by the Government on the insistence of the educated and reform-oriented women leaders. These leaders by and large did not lead independent movements but were more dependent on the government help, funding and the initiatives in framing laws and rules for women's upliftment. The National Council for Women's Education played an important rolc in spearheading the movements for women education and their upliftment. The Counsil set up a committee to examine comprehensively the problem of curricula for girls at all stages of education. This committee was set up on November 1, 1961 under the chairmanship of Smt. Hansa Mehta.

The committee after carefully examining all the evidence produced before it came to the following conclusions:

> "Our enquiry has not imbued us with any conviction that there are clear and ascertained differences between the two sexes on which an educational policy may readily be based. We have encountered a number of facile generalizations about the mental differences between boys and girls; we have found few, if any, which we are able to accept. Men and women have existed for centuries; but either sex is still a problem to the other and indeed to itself, nor is there any third sex to discriminate dispassionately between the two. In the mean time it is the part of wisdom neither to assume difference nor to postulate identity, but to leave the field free to both to show themselves".[15]

The above mentioned conclusions show the confusion in the thinking of the women leaders who failed to arrive at definite conclusions regarding the differences between two sexes. We have endeavoured to point out that such conclusions have left the field wide open for discrimination, particularly in education. The last words-but to leave the field free to both to show themselves, sounds quite traditional which emphasizes that woman's field is home and the man's work. The committee's observation may lead to the conclusion that both male and female should work freely in their own fields. However, the committee tries to refute traditional view by emphasizing that "the traditional view assumes that there are two different personalities-masculine and feminine, with widely different and complementary traits and that they owe their origin to sex. This view also has now been proved to be incorrect................ Recent scientific studies have shown that the differences in the psychological trailts of men and women are due, not to innate sex differences but to social conditioning".[16]

The committee on the basis of such observations as

above, recommend, for the education of girls and women that "Education is a great levelling force and one sure way to raising the status of women to real equality with men is to eliminate, or to reduce to a minimum, the existing wide gap in the education of girls and women."[17]

The Education Commission (1964-66) endorsed the views of the National Committee on Women's Education and emphasized:

> "The education of women should be regarded as a major programme in education for some years to come and a bold and determined effort should be made to face difficulties involved and to close the existing gap between the education of men and women in as short a time as possible".[18]

Thus we see that year after year various committees and commissions emphasized the education, of the women for raising their social status. But besides some progress in the quantitative expansion of women education no significant developments took place in raising the status of rural, down-trodden, Schedule Castes and Schedule Tribes women. Hence the committee on the Status of Women (1971-74) concentrated on this anomaly.

It observes:

> "The deep foundations of the inequality of the sexes are built in the minds of men and women through a socialization process which continues to be extremely powerful. Right from their earliest years boys and girls are brought up to know that they are different from each other and this differentiation is strengthened in every way possible—through language forms, modes of behaviour of labour etc. They begin to learn very early what is proper or not proper for boys and girls and all attempts at deviation are noticed, discouraged and sometimes punished. The sissy and the tom boy are equal objects of derision. There is nothing wrong in this if it were merely a question of distinction. But it soon gets inextricably tied up with the traditional

> concepts of the roles of men and women and their mutual relationships which are based on inequality. The process of indoctrination affects the development of individual personalities.
>
> The only institution which can counteract the effect of the process is the educational system. If education is to promote equality for women, it must make a deliberate, planned and sustained effort so that the new value of equality of the sexes can replace the traditional value system of inequality".[19]

The committee comes to the conclusion for the reasons for the variation of social attitudes and the consequent slow progress of women's education as both social and economic.

It found that a substantial number of girls are engaged in contributing to the family income by their own labour. The prevalence of child labour has been admitted as the greatest deterrent to the spread of education among children of the poor. The committee was appalled by the extent and degree of use of young girls of five to fourteen working for twelve hours a day.

The committee also found that large majority of girls by the time they reach the age of eight, are required at home to do various domestic chores, e.g., collecting fire wood, coal waste, cow dung, fetching water, at times from long distances, washing, cleaning, cooling, taking food and water to parents in their places of work etc.

About the girls education in the rural areas it observed that

> "education in the rural areas often result in alienation of the girls from their habitat. While this criticism was voiced in many places, the most vocal opinion was expressed by women in the villages of Himachal Pradesh. Since the development of the state and the standard of living of its people depended on the continued efforts of women in agriculture, education in their opinion was becoming an adversary of progress. Girls who completed their

formal education in the villages, did not want to continue living in villages or take part in agricultural activities. The problem became more acute when, owing to absence of secondary schools in the villages, they had to study outside, in urban or semi-urban areas. Many of them found village life with its hardships intolerable afterwards............ Most girls who complete secondary school develop a desire for white collared job, or urban life in some forms".

The National Policy on Education (1986) considered that "Education will be used as an agent of basic change in the status of women." It suggested that "the National Education System will play a possible interventionist role in the empowerment of women. It will foster the development of new values through redesigned curriculum, text books, the training and orientation of teachers, decision-makers and administrators, and the active involvement of educational institutions. This will be an act of faith and social engineering".

National Commission on Self-Employed Women and Women in the Informal Sector (1987-88) has emphasized:

> "Education is both an important instrument for increasing and bettering the chances of women's employability and for empowering women as they learn to think for themselves, become confident and also develop the capability of recognising more acutely the areas of exploitation."

The National Commission for Women, a statutory body was set up under the National Commission Act, 1990 to safeguard the rights and interests of women. This commission reviews legislations, intervenes in specific individual complaints of atrocities and takes remedial action to safeguard the interests of women where appropriate and feasible.

Indian Women Movement: Its Major Thrust

In Indian situation the women's movement has not been in terms of radicalism or the violent assertion of the female rights. The reason for it seems to be the sensivity of both the males and female towards the necessity of the upliftment of the women from their miserable existence. The Government and NGO all laid great emphasis on the empowerment of women for which they all recommended crash programmes for women education.

The feminist movement in India can be characterized by its sensible approach. In this movement almost all political parties except those who have leanings towards fundamentalism and orthodoxy in their outlook lend their support. By and large it is non-commercial and non-sectarian. But this movement has failed to break away from the traditional approach of motherhood, housewife and kitchen queen. The movement has not yet reached to a large section of rural and slum area women. It is the movement essentially spearheaded by urban, educated middle class. This class is in a typical paradoxical situation. It wants the best of both worlds. It wants to secure independence from male domination but is not willing to think in terms of a life pattern in which the male does not figure as a key person in the role of a father, brother or husband or in any other form.

Present Position

In spite of the feminist movements, political support and increasing awareness of evil influences on national progress of the neglect of women, we find that Indian women's status and position has not undergone any revolutionary change. No doubt the urban middle class women have become more assertive, better educated and economically independent by involving themselves in all types of jobs, some of which were so far under the special male prerogatives like those in the army, police or as airline pilots. But the majority of the women of rural and poor classes are suffering from various types of disabilities. The main reason for such a situation seem to be the woefully low percentage of female literacy. According to Prof. Moegiadi, UNESCO's representative in India "four South Asian countries Bangladesh, India, Pakistan and Nepal account for the largest number of out of school girls and illiterate women.

Addressing a national workshop on State Policies on Incentive Schemes in Primary Schools and their Contribution to Girls Participation, jointly organised by NCERT and UNESCO, he said:

> "Though progress has been made, we are all aware that according to the 1991 census of India we have 50.2 per cent literacy, and now according to the latest information we have 64 per cent literacy rate. It is estimated that in near future it can be 70-80 per cent".[20]

The number of female in the work force is also very limited. The 1991 census figures tell us that the working population was 317 millions out of the total population of the country as being 846.3 (males 439.3 and females 407.0) million. The males were 226.4 (71.4 per cent) and females 90.6 (28.6 per cent) million who were working. The males in the organized sector were 23.0 million while women were only 3.8 million. The respective percentages were 85.8 and 14.2. In the unorganized sector there were 290.2 million persons out of which 203.4 were males and 86.8 millions women. The respective percentages were 70.0 and 30.0.[21] Hence the women working in organised sector were very few as compared to men.

The National Commission on Self Employed Women and Women Engaged in Informal Sector observed that the women could be found to be largely confined to strenuous and monotonous work that might be irregular and seasonal and women workers could be rarely benefitted from the introduction of mechanization and new technology.[22] About eighty per cent of the total female work-force continues to work as agricultural labour. It may be said that one of the basic hurdles to the development of employment opportunities for the women has been lack of adequate training to women workers.

The percentage of Agricultural labourers according to 1991 census was 21.01 per cent for males and 44.83 per cent for females.[23]

Indian women are also being increasingly victimized. Crimes against women are increasing. Crimes such as rape, bride burning, wife battering and ragging of girls are also on the increase. Emotional violence against females at work is a new phenomenon.[24] The rape cases increased from 3,945 in 1982 to 97.52 in 1989. These figures are on the basis of the National Crime Records Bureau, Ministry of Home Affairs, Government of India. But the Marie Stopes Institute, Delhi thinks that these official figures are not correct. According to it on an average, two million women and girls are raped in India every year.[25]

Thus we find that even now there is much discrimination against women and they are a neglected lot. Rajbala says that "a basic statistics paints a grim picture. Over 400 million women with 75 per cent illiteracy, work 10-14 hours daily, undergo 4-6 pregnancies and run low income house holds".[26]

Present Book

In India, women have been surrounded in a web of myth and reality. She has been considered as a goddess as well as an evil incarnate. At one stage if she was put on a very high pedestal and at another stage she was thrown into the pits of filth and guilt. The casualty has been the reality of her existence. It is only recently that the emphasis has been put on the understanding of the women as she is, as also on the understanding of her relations with man in the light of the recognition of the fact that both are the equal parts of the humanity. In this context her education is now considered as important and worthwhile as that of man.

Historically, in the Indian situation the rearing of the girl child and her education has always been taken with indifference. The only exception may be the Vedic period. The birth of a male child is celebrated with joy and happiness while the birth of a girl child is a matter of sorrow and gloom for whole of the family. This trend is changing in the enlightened households but by and large in majority of the families the situation has hardly changed.

The ambivalence with which the Indian women were viewed, has created a typical situation in the relationship between men and women. It was believed that since energy resided in women, they were objects of worship. The Devi cult assigned all the creative and protective powers to women. But at the same time the women were considered as the promoters of evil, seductress who destroyed men if given freedom and the power to exercise their free will. Thus the women's will power had to be controlled. The husbands were given their absolute rights over her body, soul and mind. The women accepted their subordinate status for centuries. It is only in the later half of the twentieth century that the Indian women started revolting against the stipulations that the women are inferior to men. The empowerment of the Indian women is the battle cry of the feminists of today. The enlightened men are offering their help in the emancipation of the women.

At the advent of the new millennium we find that the Indian women are joining the world of work in increasing numbers. In many cases it is creating stresses in the family life, particularly in those homes in which the womens' role is confined to being housewives. The pressing economic demands make it obligatory for women to seek employment in various fields but the old conservative notions that the women's rightful place is in homes, create situations of stress, and conflict. Under the shadows of conflict and stress the education of the women is being planned, propagated and provided. This book highlights the conflicts and the stresses of the working as well as non-working women and also the influence of socio-psychological factors on women education.

In India, there is growing realization that the women education is of great importance to the healthy development of the social and national life. Efforts are being made to provide schools for all the girls of school-going age and to give incentives to them to learn. Still the situation is far from satisfactory. The literacy percentage among Indian women is lawfully low. This may be due to the lower social status and the psychological make up of the women, particularly of the lower classes and castes.

The Dalit women and the women of the minority communities have by and large miserable existence. The Dalit women are exploited not only by the higher caste people but also by their own male relatives. Similar is the case with the women of the minority communities, especially in the case of lower class Muslim women. The reasons for their exploitation seem to lie in their ignorance. Most of them are illiterate and so have neither the means nor the will to fight against their exploitation. Hence their education is a matter which has to be given top priority.

What will be the futuristic trends of women education? Whether women education should be of the same pattern as the education of men? If not then why and what type of education is required for them? Should women be trained for joining the world of work or only for the household work as the housewives? These are some of the questions which are being raised about women education. In the present book an attempt is being made to discuss these and some other vital issues concerning women education so that some appropriate measures may be taken for organizing women education which may usher in an era of equality, dignity, esteem, self-respect and self-confidence for the Indian women.

It may be emphasized that the issues in women education are not only confined to quantitative development. Equally important are qualitative aspects. In an article "The Burning of Roop Kanwar" Madhu Kishwar, who visited Deorala where bride burning of Roop Kanwar took place, reported that "the fascination with the sati cult has been attributed to the superstitious ignorance of illiterate village women, but it is noteworthy that the entire cult being created at Deorala is in the hands of educated men".[27] When we think of women education we are concerned with the development of progressive outlook in them. We will not like to provide that type of education to our women which the menfolk of Deorala got, which led them to close their minds rather than broadening their vision. The leaders of the pro-sati campaign were urban, educated men in their twenties and thirties.

The main premise on which the argument throughout is based is that Indian women are by nature not docile, nor are they devoid of mind of their own. It is due to four-fold major factors that we find them in the state in which they are. These factors are:

1. Religious precepts from some eminent sages motivated by the desire to subordinate the assertive women.
2. The physical weakness perpetuated by multiple pregnancies and childhood marriages.
3. Women's own desire for showering motherly affection on their own men and for maintaining domestic peace at their own cost.
4. Lastly their complete economic dependence on male-folk which has a vested interest in keeping them ignorant and illiterate.

REFERENCES

1. Rama Tai Saraswati. *The High Caste Hindu Women*, (Delhi, 1984), Reprint, Manu quoted on p. 54.
2. M.H. Kidwai, *Women under Different Social and religious Laws*, (New Delhi, 1976) quotations taken from p. 86.
3. Dorothy Mill: *The Book of the Ancient Romans*, (Lond, 1937), Cato the Censor quoted on p. 338.
4. Sister Emma Therese Healy : *Women according to Saint Bonaventure*, (New York, 1956), St. Francisian, Bonaventure quoted on p. 46.
5. Justic Sunanda Bhandare : "Society, Law and Cender Justice", in *The World of Gender Justice*, ed. by Murlidhar C. Bhandare, (New Delhi, 1999) pp. 30-31.
6. *Ibid*, p. 31.
7. *Ibid*, p. 31.
8. *Ibid*, p. 31.
9. *Ibid*, pp. 32-33.

10. *Ibid*, p. 33.
11. *Ibid*, p. 33.
12. *Report of the University Education Commission* (1948-49), New Delhi.
13. *Report of the Secondary Education Commission* (1952-53), Delhi.
14. *Report of the National Committee on Women's Education* (1958-59), Delhi.
15. *Report of the Committee Appointed by the National Council of Women's Education on the Differentiation of Curricula for Boys and Girls*, (1961), New Delhi.
16. *Ibid.*
17. *Ibid.*
18. *Report of Education Commission* (1964-66), New Delhi.
19. *Report of the Committee on the Status of Women* (1971-74).
20. Prof. Moegiadi: News Item, *The Hindustan Times*, Chandigarh, dated May 23, 2000.
21. Source: 1991 *Census* figures.
22. Raj Bala: *The Legal and Political Status of Women in India.* (New Delhi, 1999), (as reported in), pp. 142-43.
23. Source: 1991 Census figures.
24. Raj Bala, p. 182.
25. *Ibid.*
26. *Ibid.*
27. Madhu Kishwar: *Off the Beaten Track, Rethinking Gender Justice for Indian Women*, (New York, 1999), p. 59.
28. *Ibid.*

1

INDIAN WOMEN IN THE WEB OF MYTH AND REALITY

Woman has been the subject of love-hate, appreciation-ridicule, acceptance-rejection and good-evil ambivalence since ancient times. Whatever media, man had at any stage of history, used to describe and express his feelings towards women, songs were sung, dramas were staged, poems were composed, paintings were drawn, sculptures were carved, and models were constructed to concretely reveal these dichotomous emotions. Literature is full of the chaste, noblest and most revered saint-like women as well as most vile and evil witch like women. Man found woman a natural object for the satisfaction of his passion. Like food, she satisfied his natural urge and became an essential part of his existence. However, because she was a dynamic being capable of expressing her own wants and needs, man could not control her as easily as he wished. This created a frustration within him since he could neither rule her nor ignore her. Thus all of the finer and basal qualities of humanity became associated with woman. She was viewed as goddess, the representative of all that's good in human nature, and as a witch, the harbinger of all the evils in society.

In many verses of the ancient Hindu scripture, Rig Veda, women are praised as mothers and wives. In other verses, they are blamed for their evil nature. Verse 5-61-6 reads: "Yea, many a woman is more firm and better than the man who turns away from God and offers not".[1] A different view is expressed in verse 17-8-33: "The mind of woman brooks not discipline. Her intellect hath little weight."[2] A most derogatory reference to woman is found in verse 10-95-15: "With women there can be no lasting friendship: hearts of hyenas are the hearts of women."[3]

Indra cites Shatapatha Brahman as stating that women who are mothers are considered the best and foremost preceptors of children.[4] Indra further elaborates by stating that "a woman is a hundred time superior to a man in instructing and elevating a child."[5] Indra cites Manu's view that women are to be goddesses in their homes. Wives and mothers who *secure many blessings, who are worthy of worship and irradiate their dwellings* are equated to goddesses of fortune who reside in the houses of men.[6] Indra summaries Manu's views by stating that the prosperity of the family lies with the happiness of the females in the household *where the female relations live in grief, the family soon wholly perishes; the family where they are not unhappy ever prospers.* The epic *Mahabharata* enjoins all to honour women because the virtues of men depends on women and because all pleasure and enjoyments also entirely depend on them.[8]

The ambivalence with which Manu views Indian women is apparent in his description of them as morally low creatures: "It is the nature of the woman to seduce men in this world, for that reason the wise are never unguarded in the company of females. For women are able to lead! astray in this world even a learned man and make him a slave of desires and anger."[9] Women are described as lustful and impure in their desires and are debarred from receiving sacramental rites with sacred texts: "For women no sacramental rites is performed with sacred texts, thus the law is settled. Women are destitute of strength and destitute of the knowledge of Vedic texts and are as impure as falsehood itself."[10] The *Mahabharata* depicts women as deceitful and unfathomable[11]: *The faces of women are like flowers, their words are like the drops of honey and their hearts like sharp razors, the interior of them no one can know*[12]. Shukra, a writer of the post-epic age holds women as inherently weak and given to eight vices: "falsehood, inconstancy, deceitfulness, stupidity, greediness, impurity, cruelty and insolence."[13] Carstairs presents this duality in terms of the spiritualistic perception of the goddess Kali, protective mother to her worshippers. She stands on top of her male adversary, cuts off his head and drinks his blood.[14] A woman whose demands cannot be met may be viewed as one who assumes demonic powers and extracts her due. It is clear that in Indian thought the concept of protective power in women along with demonic reprisal when offended are consistently interwoven.

The *Mahabharata* attributes this fear of woman to her great sexual powers: "Fire is never satiated with fuel. Ocean can never be filled with waters that the rivers bring to it. The destroyer is never satiated with killing even all-living creatures. Likewise women are never satisfied with men."[15] Women are described as powerful, demanding, seductive and ultimately destructive. Sexual love is believed to be destructive to a man's spiritual and physical natures.

The dread of a woman's vagina is very much present in Indian culture just as it has been found in many other cultures. Horney says, "Men have never tired of fashioning expressions for the violent force by which man feels himself drawn to the woman, and side by side with his longing, the dread that through her he might die and be undone."[16] To the male Indians, the vagina was an ever opening, engulfing, unsatiable organ. They found it difficult to save themselves from the attractions of the female vagina while being afraid that upon entering it, all would be lost. They conceived it as a snatcher of their powers.

According to the famous story of the birth of Shakuntla, the great sage Vishwamitra lost his power to dislodge the heavenly king Indra as he was lured by Menka who was a celestial being of Indra's court. To lose the powers achieved after great penance is symbolically worse than physical death. Most of the Indian sages in the post-Vedic period extolled the spiritual and moral virtues of celibacy and continence. They considered that excessive physical strength could be obtained through Brahmacharya, the control of the sexual urge. Hanuman, the monkey god of the epic Ramayana, was endowed with colossal strength and became recognised as the ideal of the celibates. His strength and power were attributed to his Nitya Brahmacharya, which meant that he was able to repeal successfully the attraction of the vagina.

It was considered a crime if a woman who was in her *ritu* period was not sexually satisfied. According to the Indians, the *ritu* was twelve days after the stoppage of the flow of the menstrual fluid. This would be a woman's fertile time of ovulation. In the Epic period of India *ritu* was considered the most important part of a woman's life: *With the ritu, love begins; with it, it ends; in it, it has always its central point*".[17] The urge for coitus was supposed to be great during this time, and for a woman passing through this period, satisfaction was her holy right as well as command.

Many myths illustrate the woman arguing with a reluctant male for intercourse as if she were in her *ritu*. It was considered a sin for him not to satisfy her and give her motherhood. One such example is that of Carmishta. Devyani was the energetic daughter of a Brahmin and was married to king Yayati. Another king's daughter, Carmishta, who had insulted Devyani was given as a slave girl in marriage. Her father asked Yayati not to touch his daughter. Carmishta got her *ritu* while the king was visiting her quarters. She convinced him to make love to her on the basis of the holy law. When she complained to her father about the incident, King Yayati explained that he did not want to be known as an embryo slayer and out of that fear he went to Carmishta when she requested it of him.[18]

The leanings towards celibacy did not minimize the attraction of the vagina among the people of India. It was assigned mythical powers, in many tales where men could not be saved from its attraction. Because the entire human race sprang from this mysterious opening; it became the symbol of creation. The philosophical mind extended this symbolism to the extent that the female vagina became the goddess who created the mankind. Sculptures are available which depict the sexual triangle, the Yoni as prominently visible. Desai describes two types of these goddesses as the *opulent goddess and the personified yoni type of goddess.*[19] The *opulent goddess* has broad hips and exposed sexual triangle and is seen in a frontal pose on a pre-Asokan gold plaque of Lauriya in Champaran district.[20] The *Personified Yoni* figures existed in early centuries of the Christian era at Bhita, Jhusi and Kausambi in Uttar Pradesh, Ter and Nevasa in Maharashtra and Nagar junakonda in Andhra Pradesh. The goddess is usually headless with a lotus replacing her head. She is nude and sits with her legs apart like a frog, *Uttanapad*, with her Yoni fully visible. According to Desai, even today, *women worship such figures of the goddess and apply butter and kumkuma on the yoni for begetting children. Thus the fertility aspect of this goddess can be established beyond a doubt.*[21]

These creative powers are also associated with destructive powers, which are attributed to women. The Hindus describe earth as Mother Earth and death as a return to Mother Earth since the dead are put on the earth. Thus death is philosophically and symbolically considered a return to the womb. Horney says: *We have learned to understand the longing for death as a longing for reunion with the mother.*[22] This psycho-analytical observation is very much in keeping with the emphasis of the Hindu symbolisation of death. According to Desai, the image of the *Opulent Goddess* could have been worn as either a fertility ornament or was associated with the burial grounds. In either case, its magico-religious function is significant.[23] The vagina as a magic symbol of destruction is also implied in the curbing of sexual energy and the magical powers of chastity. In the Apastamba Dharamasutra, this view is stated: *They who keep the vow of chastity accomplish their wishes merely by conceiving them, for instance the desire to produce rain, to bestow children....*[24] This power is considered lost if the vagina is entered into.

Another factor involved in the dread of vagina is the severe restrictions placed on the menstruating women.

The Hindus believe that the presence of such a woman is offensive and the gods will not take sacrifice that she has looked upon. The food she prepares or looks upon must not be eaten, and she should not be spoken to. These taboos illustrate the fear with which ancient Indians viewed the menstrual flow as well as the fluids during and after childbirth. Some of these notions are still prevalent among a large number of illiterate and orthodox people of this country. Only the educated few have been able to transcend these myths.

It may be due to the inescapable attraction of woman that she is conversely labelled as evil in many cultures. Men can find no retreat for woman and are, therefore, led to brand her as destructive. According to the text of the Islamic Shia sect, women *are of value only as vehicles for entry into the world of spirits condemned temporarily to take on flesh in punishment for their sins; they themselves being, however, without soul.*[25]

Lederer quotes from the very revered fathers Henry Kramer and James Sprenger in Part 1, question vi, of their Malleus, 1486 AD., now *nearly all the kingdoms of the world have been overthrown by women...Therefore it is no wonder if the world suffers through the malice of women.*[26] It is said he who trusts a woman, he also trusts a deceiver. Talmund describes how God chose which part of Adam's body to make Eve from. God decided that the rib would be the chastest part, but even with all this precaution, woman has all the faults God tried to avoid. Adam, upon seeing Eve, said, *This is my never silent Hell.*

Christian sages regarded woman as evil. Tertulliam wrote the following for the edification of his contemporaries:

> "You must know that you are Eve. You are the devil's gateway... How easily you destroyed man, the image of God. Because of the death which you brought upon us, even the Son of God had to die."[28]

Women are viewed differently in Hindu religion in that the Hindus branded women as goddesses possessing energy. The Shakti or power is embodied in the female and not in the male. Man alone is not the beginning and end. Man without woman is nothing. *Maya Shakti is personified as the world protecting feminine, maternal side of the Ultimate Being, and as such, stands for the spontaneous, loving acceptance of life's tangible reality.*[29] Thomas Aquinas on the other hand says, *In a secondary sense the image of God is found in man, and not in woman: for man is the beginning and the end of every creature.*[30] *The Hindus personify the energy of a God and speak of* it as his wife (Shakti). *Not separate from Himself, for a better understanding of the active aspect of the deity, she is brought within the compass of human perceptive capacity and endowed with an entity of her own*[31], states P. Thomas.

In spite of this recognition of the female as active principle, the Indian male failed to continue to revere and respect woman. Instead he became obsessed with controlling and subduing her. Except in the Vedic times and the Epic times, women were always ill-treated. With the passage of time, a wide gulf was created between the spiritual aspect of woman's existence and her physical being. Traditional observance to the goddess replica of woman was continued while, in reality, her status and power within society and the family was continually undermined. Eventually, women were considered mere possessions and burned alive with their deceased husbands. The Indian woman lost her image as a goddess and her witch nature became the standard of belief.

The process of subjugating the virile, strong Aryan women was difficult task. The assertive male had to search out many means by which to accomplish this domination. She had to be pulled down from her goddess pedestal. This was accomplished by completely domesticating her. She was taught that she must keep harmony in the family and submit completely to her husband's wishes. If she worshipped her husband as lord and master, then she might regain her status and be put again on her throne. The myths, stories and preaching of the sages put forth an intense psychological impression upon the mind of the woman and brain washed her into a life of secondary existence. Horney highlights this phenomenon in her essay,

The Dread of Woman, in which she discusses the fears that men have of women which might have contributed to the male originated concept of penis envy which may have been defensively constructed to bolster a threatened ego. Kelman agrees with this in the introduction of this book:

> "Throughout history man has seen woman as a sinister and mysterious being, particularly dangerous when she is menstruating. Man attempts to deal with his dread by denial and defiance...Men deny their dread by love and adoration and defend themselves from it by conquering, debasing and diminishing the self-respect of women."[32]

In the Indian context, men express their dread of women by first giving them supernatural powers as goddesses. Then they defend themselves by weaving an intricate web of mythology around chastity and sub-servience. Thus, women were put under constant surveillance by either their parents, or husbands and even by their sons. The ancient law giver Manu was of the opinion that *Her father protects her in childhood, her husband protects her in youth and her son protects her in old age: a woman is never fit for independence.*[33]

Juanita Williams summarizes a number of myths that have been used to categorize women. She says: *There is woman as earth mother, a fertile creature who is somehow more in tune with nature than is her male counterpart. Then there is woman as seductress, another magical creature whose charms lure the man away from the narrow path of rectitude and responsibility.*[34]

Education of Women

Due to ambivalence regarding the women's status and position in the Indian culture, society and philosophy her education was not given proper attention in various periods of the history of India except perhaps in the Vedic period. The Rig Vedic society was founded on the base of home and family with the proper place assigned to women under an advanced system of material laws. There was no seclusion of women and consequently no Purdah. Aryan taught their women music and dancing, the religious lore and warfare, literature, fine arts and languages.

During the Upanishad period women enjoyed an equal eminence with men. The two sexes were considered as the two wheels of the same chariot. The women received domestic education. She also learnt the art or some handicrafts. She was taught the elements of hygiene, physiology, and nutrition along with literature, language, fine arts, etc.

The women of Ramayana and Mahabharata were given proper opportunities for education. Women like men were entitled to Upanayana or initiation into Brahamcharya or Vedic studentship. Women were versed not only in the highest philosophy but also in the other branches of knowledge.

During Buddhism there was acceptance of female education, including religious and spiritual education. It opened a new gate for the salvation of women. But Lord Buddha never thought women to be fit for ruling a nation as they were thought to be easy victims of the senses, passion, anger, hate, greed, etc.

Jainism believed that there were very few women who had strength of mind and body adequate to study the faith and to endure the hard life of an ascetic. Men were considered more physically fit than women for undertaking a course of self-mortification and self-effacement.

The invasion on India by the Muslims brought about deterioration in the position of the women. Restrictions on her freedom and rights were imposed. Muslim women were practically denied access to learning. Excluded from worshipping with the men, they were excluded from the mosques where most education occurred and also from the Kuttabs and Madarasah system. Essentially, woman's education and training, the Muslims maintain should be confined to their domestic and nurturing functions so as to make them more useful to their families and homes.

At the time when the Indians came in vital contact with the British in the later half of the eighteenth-century, the position of the Indian women had reached the maximum degree of degeneration. But the European usherance brought breath of fresh air. The close contacts with Western cultural traditions, literature and education had deep impact on the minds of Indian leaders. The result was that a number of social reform movements started in the nineteenth century. These resulted in a strong movement for the emancipation of women. Thus the pre-independence period marked the beginning of the awareness of the oppressive social customs which had reduced the status of a woman to that of a slave. The advent of Mahatma Gandhi stimulated women to fight for their honourable existence. This period in India may be described as a period of renaissance for the Indian womanhood. During this period there was a revolt against the Purdah system and fight against the old and established but decadent conventions.

India won her independence in 1947. Soon after this, Indian Constitution was framed and adopted in 1950. The women were granted equal status and position under Article 14 of the Constitution. But still the women were not able to achieve their rightful place in the social set-up. Customs, traditions and the myths ingrained through centuries of prejudice continued to operate to prevent women from exercising their rights and from benefiting from whatever opportunities were offered to them. One of the basic reasons for this was the mass illiteracy among Indian women. It is well-recognized that in the struggle for empowerment of women education plays the most significant role. In India women education was, by and large, neglected till very recently. Why has this happened? It is the main theme of the present book. The book concentrates on the socio-psychological dimensions of women education, mainly, in a historical perspective.

The socio-psychological dimensions refer to the socio-psychological make-up of the women and the cultural factors responsible for their status and position in the society. The socio-psychological make-up involves the attitudes, aspirations, motivations, interests etc.

In the following Chapters the duties and obligations

assigned to women, the norms of conduct expected of them, and the ideal to be achieved by them, and the role of education in equipping them for their obligations are being discussed.

REFERENCES

1. Prof. Indra, *The Status of Women in Ancient India*, (Lahore, 1940).
2. Mildreth Worth Pinkham, *Woman in the Sacred Scriptures of Hinduism*, (New York, 1951), p. 21.
3. Pinkham, p. 21.
4. Indra, pp. 3-4.
5. Indra, p. 4.
6. Indra, p. 5.
7. Indra, pp. 5-6.
8. Indra, pp. 6-7.
9. Indra, p. 14.
10. Indra, p. 15.
11. Indra, pp. 15-17.
12. Indra, pp. 18-19.
13. Indra, p. 19.
14. G.M. Carstairs' *The Twice Born*, (Bloomington, 1958), p. 157.
15. Indra, p. 15.
16. Karen Horney, *Feminine Psychology*, (New York, 1967), p. 134.
17. John Jakob Meyer, *Sexual Life in Ancient India: A Study in the Comparative History of Indian Culture*, (New York, 1930), p. 216.
18. Meyer. p. 222.
19. Devangana Desai: *Erotic Sculpture of India: Socio-cultural Study*. (New Delhi, 1975), p. 10.
20. Desai, p. 10.
21. Desai, p. 12.
22. Horney, p. 117.
23. Desai, p. 10.
24. Desai, p. 102.

25. Wolfgang Lederer, *The Fear of Women*, (New York, 1968), p. 168.
26. Lederer, p. 208.
27. Lederer, p. 75.
28. Mary Daby, *The Church and the Second Sex*, (New York, 1968), p. 45.
29. Heinrich Zimmer, *Myths and Symbols in Indian Art and Civilization*, (New York, 1946), p. 25.
30. Daby, p. 50.
31. P. Thomas, *Epics, Myths and Legends of India*, (Bombay, 1961), p. 54.
32. Horney, p. 20.
33. Manu quoted in Pandita Ramabai Saraswati: *The High Caste Hindu Women*, (New Delhi, Inter Indian Publications, 1984), pp. 50-54.
34. J.H. Williams, *Psychology of Women: Behaviour in a Biosocial Context*, (New York, Norton, 1977).

2

LOSS OF WILL POWER: DENIAL OF EDUCATION

As centuries rolled on Aryan culture was firmly entrenched in this land. Indian women were trapped more and more in the web of myth and lost their sense of self and will. The goddesses were robbed of their glory even though they were still seated on a high pedestal. Men's obsession was to pull them down to earth by having the women sing their praises and do their will. Only when the women pleased them and satisfied their ego-needs, did they call them the goddesses of the household (*Girhya Lakshmi*). The moment women defied male idiosyncrasies, they were called devils. Men took upon themselves the responsibilities of protecting and feeding the women who were consequently destitute and completely dependent. The women were not allowed to move outside the household without male company since it was taken for granted that they were incapable of defending themselves. Women became frail and weak creatures and believed that if any man other than their husbands touched them or cast a lustful glance towards them they were defiled and dishonoured. Hence, their only path to an honourable existence was to give the men unflinching loyalty, submit to their care and deny their own self and will.

Perhaps in no other culture does such a duality exist where women have been mythically placed upon a high pinnacle while at the same time pulled down to dust in reality. In no other civilisation the women's status in the social milieu has been raised so high and simultaneously, so brutally lowered as in the Indian culture. In other cultures women are usually labelled as either saint or sinner, while in India she is both. Years of being enmeshed in the many strands of this web have deeply affected the position of the Indian women.

Women of the early Aryan civilisation were highly respected. This society, however, as patriarchal, therefore, the birth of a girl was generally an unwelcome event.[1] As early as in 2000 BC charms and rituals ensured the birth of a son in preference to that of a daughter. These charms are reported in the ancient *Atharva Veda*. Even though a son was desired and preferred, the birth of a daughter was not a source of great consternation to the family. Alteker points out that some scholars of this period were of the opinion that a gifted and well-mannered daughter might be a source of pleasure to the family. No restrictions were placed on girls in performing religious rites. The marriage of a daughter was not a difficult problem since she was free to choose her husband.[2]

The marriage of girls used to take place at the age of 16 or 17 years.[3] The women were not restricted and were allowed freedom of movement within the society, even in the company of their lovers. The wife occupied the honoured place in the family as the mistress of her household. Marriages were mostly monogamous. Widow remarriage was usually permitted within the family.[4] Parents desired their daughters to marry the husbands of their choice. During the early Vedic period, the prayer of an anxious father used to be "May *Saviter* lead and bring to thee the husband whom thy heart desires".[5] Pinkham notes: It is important for us to note that a wife was on a level of equality at the hearth which was the altar of sacrifice.[6]

Around 1500 BC, the education of the daughters confined to the family. Religious and secular training was given only to girls from rich and cultured families. Men performed functions in the religious sacrificial rites, which had previously been the wife's domain. Girls were married at about the age of sixteen years, and divorce and widow remarriage were still permitted.[7]

Gradually circumstances changed. As ancestor worship gained popularity, sons alone were permitted to perform religious rites. Women became "valued only as the vehicles for bearing sons, and when they were unfit or unwilling to perform this function, they were considered useless".[8] The value of the sons increased further, and they began to be regarded as investments for the future. Without a son, no man or woman could hope to go to heaven.[9] The position of the daughter was greatly undermined. Still the women were not debarred from the study of the Vedas and there existed very few taboos regarding the rearing of girls.

During the Epic period in India, the birth of daughter became an exceedingly negative event because of the prevalence of marriage customs, which subordinated the position of women. Still, a daughter was regarded as a prized possession, and family took a keen interst in her rearing. In Mahabharata, Draupadi is described as the common property of the five brothers. She was put at stake in a gambling bout. Sita, the ideal woman character of Ramayana, was put to fire ordeal to prove her chastity. She was denounced by Lord Rama to prove himself as an deal king. Draupadi did not accept her subordinate position and fought in an open assembly when Duryodhana the winner of the bout, sought to derobe her. Sita, on the other hand, took her humiliations with fortitude and goodwill toward her husband. However, by this time the right of the husband over his wife or a man over a woman was generally accepted by the society irrespective of whether women acknowledge it willingly or not.

This willing acceptance, even today, is considered as the ideal of womanhood. Sita is worshipped in most of the devout homes for her absolute obedience to her husband. Everywhere in India her example is exalted to be followed by all women. Sita had great strength of character and virtue. She pursued what she considered to be right. Her love for the husband was limitless. Her character was of utmost purity and chastity. If we for the sake of argument forget for the time being the divinity of Rama and Sita there arises a doubt in our minds that such a character might have been drawn to satisfy the male ego by the male poets. It might be possible that Sita's character was enfolded in the myth of male supremacy and female subordination so that the women's sole aspiration in life became the loyalty and the service to her husband who was put at the level of God to her. This emphasis on chastity and service to the husband may lead to the conclusion that the women of this period were put on pedestal as goddesses only if they lived the ideal and the virtuous life according to the most rigid standards set by a male dominated society.

The witch type of the nature of women is demonstrated in the Ramayana through the story about Kaikeyi and Manthra. Kaikeyi tried through deceit to obtain the throne for her son. Manthra prompted her to do so. Hence both are branded as great culprits at the opposite end of the spectrum from Sita.

An aspect worth noticing in the character portrayal of Mahabharata heroines is the strong willed woman. They are depicted as "resolute, full of fire, passionate in comparison with the often slackened, spineless men"[10]. Perhaps the Indians of this period were not in full control of their women and were frustrated enough to seek means of controlling them. One such means was to put an exceedingly high value on loyalty and chastity. Meyer points out that in Indian literature no ideal of a man is found; however, idealistic character portrayals of women are outstanding, especially in the Epic period[11]. We may not entirely agree with this view as the portrayal of characters of Shri Rama, Shri Krishna and other heroes of Epic period cannot be ignored and yet there seems to be truth in this observation that women of this period were certainly of strong will.

During the post-Vedic period, the age of marriage of girls was nine or ten years. Since the marriage was performed at such a young age, the choice then was not that of the girl but of the parents or other elders. A woman was debarred from revoking her marriage but the husband was free to throw his wife out of his household if she was not submissive. Widow marriage became unacceptable and was banned by 500 AD. The dictum that "the wife ought to revere her husband as a god even if he was vicious and void of any merit was accepted as applying to all women"[12]. The Law of Manu became the accepted way of life. It stated that the father should protect his daughter while she was young, her husband when she was married, and her son when her husband was no longer there. This law contributed to woman's inferior status in society and denied her all decision making rights[13].

Kautilya was in favour of marrying girls at a tender age. He advocated the marriage of girls when menses appear. He advocated the punishment of parents who did not marry their daughters at proper time. According to Jha: "Probably Kautilya advocates early marriage with a view to maintaining the chastity of girls, preventing women from joining nunneries, check love marriages, utilising the fertile period of girls for bringing forth offspring, and increasing the population at a time when frightful wars of conquest reduced Hindu population by one-half".[14] Kautilya propagates the subjection of women in married life. The wife must remain under the control of her husband. As the girls; were to be married at an early age their education was totally neglected. Kautilya considered that a wife must be fully devoted to her husband and blindly follow him. The woman's freedom of speech was totally curbed and since her individuality was denied she was kept ignorant.

At this time, Buddhism developed in India as a revolt against Brahmanism, a too formal ritualistic religion prevalent about six centuries before the birth of Christ, Buddhism soon spread throughout India and dominated the nation until about 800 AD. Buddhists still maintained women in an inferior position through an emphasis on celibacy for men who made women appear unclean or as objects simply for men's pleasure. Women were admitted to the Buddhist order as a gradual change occurred.

According to Altekar, this change was the beginning of a movement, which led to new attitudes about female education among ladies in commercial and aristocratic familes[15]. Several ladies from Buddhist families led lives of celibacy with the aim of understanding and following the eternal truths of religion and philosophy. Some women like Sanghamitra went to foreign countries to propagate Buddhism. Also, many women of the Jaina faith devoted their time to learning and became famous scholars. However, these were early exceptions. For the majority of women, no educational gains were made between 300 AD and 800 AD because of either Buddhism or Jainism[16]. The celibate Jaina monks considered women as the temptresses that perpetuated the misery that was life[17]. This attitude certainly did not deter in general the Jainas from marriage or begetting of children. Women were given place of honour in the household. However, the monkish tales about celibacy did contribute to ambivalence among the Jaina men in their behaviour pattern with their women. Jaina men enjoyed their women in spite of the religious discourses about their evils.

The road back to educational equality was slow and difficult. By 500 AD the religious influence had obligated all education for women. The model women were exposed to remodelled. Women were exposed to such literature, which highlighted dependence and punishment for breaking the norms of conduct imposed on them by indifferent priests. A blind faith developed among the women through a process of awe and forced reverence[18]. The Puranic literature cites examples where the husband was carried on his wife's shoulders to the house of a prostitute. The wife's willingness to put her husband's needs above hers proved that she was a sati[19].

This literature which seems to have been developed by male Hindu priests completely subjugated the will of women. It emphasised husband worship along with the notion that a woman's salvation was possible only by doing that which her husband desired. An abundance of stories about *Pativarta Nari* or the husband worshipping woman influenced women to perform every kind of unnatural act for the sake of their husbands. Women started taking pleasure in their morbid existence. Eventually they became even greater fanatics than men in opposing their freedom. Perhaps they were so removed from the idea of an independent existence that even the thought of such responsibility frightened them. It may be said that it is human nature that one wants to stay with the familiar even if it is destructive because the unknown is scary.

Muslims considered marriage as a contract. In certain respects, the Muslim law gave woman a higher position in the society than the medieval Hindu law. However, the *purdah* or veil as well as the women's ignorance of the law diminished this small difference[20]. The Muslim men believed that their women would remain safe only if they were not exposed to temptation. Thus the women were denied the right to make choices.

The Muslims like Hindus believed that the women's only path to salvation lay in the service to their menfolk. Divorce was shunned and many myths were woven about the dutiful wife who was prepared to sacrifice her all for her husband. Muslim had put all types of restrictions on the movement of their women outside their households and by and large they were restricted from having any contact with men who did not belong to their immediate family. Chastity was valued and the husband considered it his conjugal duty to keep his wife away from temptation.

According to the Holy Quoran women were respected because they bore children. Progeny was very important to the Muslims as defenders in warfare against unbelievers. Hence among Muslims there also developed ambivalent feelings towards their women. Women were respected for being mothers but at the same time they were restricted from having any freedom of action. They were completely subjugated by the dominant males. Due to a number of environmental factors affecting the Indian Muslims the feelings of respect were overcome by the need or restriction. Most of the legal rights of the women were virtually subjected to the male will.

The early Muslim period was one of great instabilities. Local feuds and conversions were dominating the social life. The fanaticism and religious intolerance closed the doors to rationality. The women were the worst sufferers of the irrationality of the ignorant priests and religious fanatics. Their spirit of inquiry was crushed, as they were not allowed any interaction with learned or open minded persons. The women were left with no option but to submit to their submissive role and suffer indignities and cruelties in silence. Dubey describes the personality and the character of the women that emerged during this period: "They had no status in society; none in their own estimation. They were more like puppets, which move when someone pulls the strings than individual human beings with minds of their own[21].

At this time the patriarchal type of family in its perfectly developed state was generally in existence. The senior male in the family was the undisputed head. Hindu women could not claim any patronage since the law of succession did not give them independent right of inheritance. The inheritor of the property was made responsible for looking after the widow of the deceased. However, in spite of their low social status, women were still the ideal of conjugal devotion, and the family was the most intimate and enduring social relationship. Dubey considered that "the Hindu family was an ideal family, the Hindu parents....Mothers were not equalled by any people on the earth in tenderness towards their progeny and attachment to the family ties"[22].

This attachment to their families was not an exercise of free will for the women. They only knew to be dutiful wives and loving mothers. No other options were open to them. In most cases, motherhood was the only solace for them in their subordinate existence. As mothers, they elicited respect, and through their sons, they ruthlessly made attempts to dominate their daughter-in-laws and other poor and dependent relatives. The condition of the women in the Indian society continued to remain low. The disruption of the Mughul Empire in the eighteenth-century and the consequent confusion throughout the country added to the women's miseries. At the beginning of British rule, the marriage age was lowered to three or four years. Since hygienic conditions were poor and disease and famine were common, a large number of girls became widows in their early childhood. These child widows were ill treated and considered a curse to their families.

The use of the veil became popular, particularly among the Muslims. The higher-class women were kept away from the males by means of *purdah*. Even a glimpse of a woman's fully clothed and veiled body by a stranger was not tolerated. While travelling, dark clothes also covered the vehicle, and when the women entered it and left it, the male servants or the carriers had to be removed from their presence.

The observance of *purdah* was not only to safeguard the honour and chastity of women, it also kept them for special pleasure of the men. Certainly, the veil produced a special type of feminine beauty, which was pale and passionate with mystic eyes, and the mind of a child. Such women seemed to appeal to the morbid taste of the pleasure lovers. When a woman is unlimited and has free social interaction with the opposite sex, her sexual impulses are toned down. Perhaps those who put their women in *purdah* do so to obtain more sexual pleasure out of them.

During the period of Muslim rule, quite a number of upper caste Indian widows burned themselves on the funeral pyres of their husbands. This was known as the *sati* system. The Sanskrit word *sati* means "true wife" or "good woman." Thus a woman was considered true to her husband when she burned her body with him after his death. Akbar, the Mughal emperor, made efforts to stop this practice about 1600 AD. He, however, was unsuccessful. When the British became the rulers, they found this practice so firmly entrenched that they also had no luck in disrupting it. The magnitude of the tradition is further understood by noting that in the year 1803, 275 women were burned at their husbands' funeral pyres within 30 mile radius of Calcutta. Within six months of the year 1804 in the same area, the number was 115.[23]

The British passed an Act in 1829 to stop the burning of widows. However, the practice continued in rural parts of India as late as 1905 when a few people participated in a *sati* ceremony in Bihar and were condemned to prison[24]. The Hindu priesthood strongly resisted the British India law. They argued that Vedas, their holy text, sanctioned the practice, therefore, alien rulers could not suppress this practice. When the religious texts were examined, it was found that the Hindu priests had falsified them to support this rite. The prevalence of the *sati* system and the opposition of its abolition by the orthodox priests show the extent to which a society can degenerate in the name of religious law. It also shows the strong influence of myth which the men and women came to believe. The honour of a family became so strongly linked with the widow burning that the kinsmen of a widow could cruelly push her into the fire. Unfortunately, the abolition of *sati* system did not end the miseries of the Hindu widows. Their burning was stopped, but they were still treated worst than the pet animals of the household. They were not allowed to remarry and had to pass their lives depending on the charity of their kinsmen and serving them like domestic servants. The plight of the young widows was extremely bad.[25] They were not only tortured but also many times sexually exploited by the unscrupulous males in the family or the neighbourhood.

Unfortunately *sati* system is still not completely wiped out. In September 1987, a young widow of 18 years Roop Kanwar was burnt at the funeral pyre of her deceased husband, a bare seven months after her wedding. The burning took place before a large gathering of people. The illiterate village folk endorsed the *sati pratha* and the rural women developed worshipful attitude toward the burnt widow. She became a deity. The myth woven centuries ago around the virtuous wives and self-destroying satis as goddesses seemed to persist in the minds of the people. It is worth noticing that all those women and men who supported and organised the burning of Roop Kanwar were not totally illiterate. They were some that were educated. Yet the type of education which they had received did not result in opening the vistas of their minds. This has in fact opened the question of quality of education, which these persons had received. In the case of these persons education which they had received had completely failed in developing in them a positive attitude towards modernity and a will to fight against orthodoxy perpetuated by a corrupt and ill-informed priestly class.

The institution of prostitution continued to flourish as a respectable way of life and the dancing girls were patronised by the nobles and landowners of their villages or towns. Chakraborty writes that in 1853, the Chief Magistrate of Calcutta reported that his town with its 416,000 people supported 12,419 such women. Of these upwards of 10,000 were Hindus, including several daughters of the Kulin Brahmins[26].

Existing along with the customary form of prostitution, which was quite common in most of the country there was another form of prostitution that of Devdasi cult or temple prostitution. In early times, the practice of offering virgins to the deity was common. Some examples can also be found in the temple precincts of Sumerian culture in Mesopotamia. In India, the Dravidians who may have borrowed it from Egypt or Mesopotamia probably introduced this custom. In the Rig Veda there is a clear reference to the dancing girl. Usha, the goddess of dawn, is compared to a dancing girl wearing embroider garments and baring her bosom[27]. In the Atharva Veda there is also a reference to the existence of women called Gandharva grihtas (possessed or owned by Gandharvas). They do not marry and exist for the pleasure of gods and men.

The cult of Devadasi originated in the early civilisation and became prevalent in South India between the sixth and the thirteenth centuries AD. During the reigns of Pallavas and Cholas all big temples recruited girls for temple prostitution. The temple dancers were married to the temple deity at a young age. They were taught music, dancing and the classical literature. After seven years of practice, the rite of worship of anklets (*gajjai puja*) took place. This was the first wearing of the anklets for the dancer[28]. It has been traditional for families to offer their daughters as Devadasis or servants of the gods. In spite of the Devadasi Protection Act of 1934, some families still continue with this tradition in Maharashtra and Karnataka. In most other parts of India, this practice has been abolished.

The courtesan in India has filled a need for the men, which the wives were unable to meet. It seemed normal to a wealthy male that wives are kept for progeny and prostitutes for pleasure both sexually and aesthetically. The high-class courtesans throughout most of India's history were the most learned women in the country. Santosh Chatterjee in one of his articles has observed that "Be she of heaven or this earth, the courtesan in India had dual purposes in her life. She was in one way an object of lust for men, in another way she was the repository of all the delightful acts of music, dancing and personal decoration"[29].

The cult of Devadasis supported the envelopment of women in the web of myth regarding self-sacrifice and negation of will for men's pleasure. Women lost their individuality due partly to the contrivance of men and partly due to their need for the advantages they gained by being submissive.

Many factors contributed to women's dependent state. Numerous pregnancies during her most active years left her unfit and unable for engaging themselves in any type of employment except in the case of very poor or destitute women. Men accepted the responsibility of looking after the material needs of the women but in return for this they demanded from them unflinching loyalty and devotion. They denied them any opportunity to develop them physically or mentally or to develop their own will power. Thus women became weak and inferior to men as human beings. This degeneration of the women in India was at its peak by the end of the eighteenth century. By the beginning of the nineteenth century the entrapment of the women in the mythical web was so complete that in almost all the spoken languages of India women were described as evil, an appendage of men, and always open to temptation.

And so such sayings were quoted:

"To educate a women is like placing a knife in the hands of a monkey"[30].

"Where there are women, there is trouble"[31].

"Woman is a poisonous creeper, avoid her company; her love destroys faith, caste, wealth and money"[32].

"He who is guilty of sin easily begets daughters"[33].

REFERENCES

1. A.S. Altekar, *The Position of Women in Hindu Civilization*, (Delhi, 1962), p. 3.
2. A.S. Altekar, pp. 3-4.
3. S.C. Dubey. "Men's and Women's Roles in India: A Sociological Review, in *Women in the New Asia*. Ed. By Barbara Ward. (Paris, 1963), p. 183.
4. S.C. Dubey, p. 184.
5. Padmini Sengupta, *The Story of Women of India*, (New Delhi, 1974), p. 55.
6. Mildreth Pinkham, *Women in the Sacred Scriptures of Hinduism*, (New York, 1941), p. 18.
7. Dubey, pp. 184-85.
8. Thomas, *Indian Women through the Ages*, (New York, 1964), p. 54.
9. Thomas, p. 54.
10. Johann Jakob Meyer. *Sexual Life in Ancient India: A Study in the Comparative History of Indian Culture*, (New York, 1930), pp. 437.
11. Meyer, p. 437.
12. Dubey, p. 186.
13. Pinkham, p. 76.
14. B.K. Jha: "The Position of Women in the Arthashastra," in C.M. Agrawal (ed.): *Dimensions of Indian Womanhood*, (Vol.), (Almora, 1993), p. 8.
15. Altekar, p. 12.
16. *Ibid.*, p. 17.
17. Thomas, p. 110.

18. Dubey, p. 188.
19. K.M. Kapadia, *Marriage and family in India*, (London, 1966), p. 169.
20. Thomas, p. 246.
21. Dubey, p. 189.
22. Raghuvanshi, *Indian Society in the Eighteenth Century*, (New Delhi, 1969), p. 91.
23. William Fielding, *Strange Customs of Courtship and Marriage*, (New York, 1942), p. 90.
24. Fielding, p. 91.
25. Usha Chakraborty, *Condition of Bengali Women around Second Half of the 19th century*, (Calcutta, 1963), p. 17.
26. Chakraborty, p. 25.
27. Vithal Nadkarni, "Devadasis-Married to God and Mammon," The *Illustrated Weekly of India*, 12-14-20, p. 75.
28. Nadkarni, p. 75.
29. *Ibid.*, p. 75.
30. Selwyn Gurney Champion, *Racial Proverbs: A Selection of the World's Proverbs Arranged Linguistically*, (New York, 1938), p. 405.
31. Champion, p. 405.
32. *Ibid.*, p. 409.
33. *Ibid.*, p. 421.

3

REALITY AND AWAKENING

The nineteenth century in India may be noted for the most abominable conditions for women as well as the initiation of their emancipation. At the beginning of the century, the women were humiliated and tortured, kept illiterate, tradition bound and in complete subjugation to the men's will. As time passed, people began to rebel against this state of affairs.

The impact of western culture created a desire among many Indians to examine their beliefs and ideals. The scientific approach of the west initiated a search of Indian scriptures and mythologies for the causes of maladies that existed in society. A critical outlook among educated Indians aided the reinterpretation of religious texts, and rational approaches replaced emotional reaction. These approaches led to the conclusion that blind faith, inability to discern right from wrong, and propagation of erroneous interpretations by decadent priestly class and immoral feudal lords had all been responsible for the existing web of subordination around women.

Reformers began their work in the direction of women's emancipation in the late nineteenth century. This work was continued in the twentieth century. In spite of great zeal and enthusiasm, the reformers achieved little success in breaking the strong notions of women's inferior status. However, the process of awakening to reality was initiated and India passed to an era in which myth around women began to be seriously questioned in terms of realities of human existence. Women started regaining their freedom of will and intellect. Still with the majority of women a major problem remained. They had for long believed that they were emotionally, morally, biologically and intellectually inferior to men and so were unable to contemplate their equal status with men. They failed to realise their full potential and high abilities. To alter this situation it was required that not only women, but the whole society should undergo a transition in its outlook towards them.

Let us now examine the movement for the emancipation of women, which was initiated in the nineteenth century.

It was largely through the efforts of Raja Ram Mohan Roy (1774-1833) that in 1829 Lord Bentinck decreed for the abolition of the sati system. He worked towards widow remarriages, inter-caste and inter-racial marriages, abolition of child marriages and polygamy. He founded a new religious order called the Brahmo Samaj. This reformed order became well known for the privileges it gave to women.[1]

Keshab Chandra Sen (1838-1884) became Roy's spiritual successor and worked tirelessly for women's education. The Civil Marriage Act III of 1872 raised the minimum age for marriage to fourteen, gave permission for widow remarriage and inter-caste marriage and penalised polygamy. This reform was applicable only to members of the Brahmo Samaj and was brought: about by Sen's courage and perseverance.[2]

Many other prominent Indians were motivated by the example set by Keshab Chandra Sen. They led a vigorous struggle against: child marriage and advocated widow remarriages. Ganga Ram at Lahore, along with others, started campaigns for women's emancipation. Mahadev Govinda Ranade (1842-1901) led a movement in Poona. He was a great patriot and social reformer who worked against existing Hindu customs, which made the life of the Indian women one of sorrow and hardship. It is notable that his reforms started with his own wife whom he taught himself.

In the north, Swami Dayanand Saraswati (1827-1883) founded a religious order named Arya Samaj. The basic tenet of this order advocated equality of opportunity for all irrespective of caste, colour, or sex. In a very active manner, this society worked for women's education. Dayanand broadened the scope of women's education by emphasising education for self rather than linking it to their efficiency in familial roles. The curriculum for education devised by Dayanand was similar for both boys and girls. Hence Dayanand emerged as the first reformer who advocated and evolved a comprehensive scheme of education for raising women's status not only at the level of family and society but for her own development as an individual.[3]

Another prominent person of the nineteenth century, Ishwar Chandra Vidyasagar (1820-1891) helped the British Government to establish the first girl's school in Calcutta in 1849. He was further responsible for the establishment of forty girls' schools in Bengal between 1855-1858. The Government Act of 1856, which legalised widow remarriage for Hindu women, was passed largely because of his efforts.

A brilliant national leader Gopala Krishna Gokhale (1866-1915) worked relentlessly towards raising the status of women in Indian society. He founded "Servants of India Society" in 1905 and established as its main objective the education of women. Two religious leaders who helped in bringing about the renaissance in the Hindu religion were Rama Krishna Paramahansa (1833-1866) and Swami Vivekananda (1862-1902).[4]

Pandita Ramabai (1858-1922) was the most prominent of women of the nineteenth century who fought the battle for her own and her sisters' emancipation. Her book *The High Class Hindu Woman* was published in 1888 and highlighted the burdensome life of the caste Hindu women. She made a fervent appeal to the American (men and women) to render help for the emlightenment of Indian women and society. The last words of her book state:

> "In the name of humanity, in the name of your sacred responsibilities as workers in the cause of humanity, summon you, true women and men of

America, to bestow your help quickly, regardless of nation, caste or creed."[5]

American admirers sent Ramabai Rs.6000 to aid a widows' home, Sharda Sadan (home of learning), which she opened.

Another woman closely associated with education for women was Ramabai Ranade (1865-1922) who was the wife of Justice Ranade. She established an educational institution called *Seva Sadan*. Anandibai Joshi (1865-1887) was the first Hindu woman to take a Degree of Doctor of Medicine in America. Because she died very young, she could not provide a much-needed influence on education in medicine for Indian women. However, her life and work inspired women of late nineteenth and early twentieth centuries. Francina Sorabji (1833-1907) with her daughters, particularly her fifth daughter Cornelia planned and organised the establishment of schools for girls in the Western region of India. Cornelia was awarded a Law Degree from England.

Mohan Das Karamchand Gandhi, a shrewd politician and advocate of the righteous path, raised his voice against injustices to women of India in the 1920's. He took up many causes, including widow remarriage and drew many women into his fight for freedom. His writings, speeches and private advocacy of the women's cause were attended to with great respect. In an article in a publication called *Young India* on November 18, 1926 he made it clear that if a man could remarry after the death of his spouse, a woman should also have this right: "What is considered desirable for man should be equally so for woman, and therefore, a widow should have the discretion as widowers about remarriage".[6] In the same article he made the following comments:

> "I look to every youth in India to' resolve not to marry a girl under sixteen. ——Let us tear down Purdah with one mighty effort. ———All that I have said about the wife applies equally——to the husband———. She is a co-sharer with him of equal——rights and of equal duties."[7]

Gandhi's approach towards women was idealistic. Though he was aware of their woes, he didn't think they had the same failings as men. He believed that their potential goodness incapacitated by years of bondage would, once freed, alleviate all the ills of society. He wrote that woman is sacrifice personified.[8] His ideal of love was feminine as he identified the greatest asset of a female as the ability to give motherly love. He saw the family as the nucleus of all Social Life and believed that women best functioned at home rather than in the work-force. He saw the ideal of women with strong characters tending their families with peace and harmony and leading the world in this direction. He addressed a meeting of mill workers in 1920 at Ahmedabad:

> "It is not for women to work in factories. They have plenty of work in their own homes. They should attend to the bringing up of their children. If women go to work, our social life will be ruined and moral standards will decline".[9]

Although Gandhi's efforts favoured the traditional role for women, he believed they deserved equal recognition for a job well done, just as men received. Gandhi's struggle for women's rights was that of dignity and humanity, rather than one of role differentiations. Certainly, in the tradition bound society into which his ideas were received they were quite revolutionary. His zeal led people to a realisation of injustices to women and prepared men to be more realistic in their attitudes towards women.

However, Gandhi still maintained the goddess image on a pedestal while exploding the myths about the witch like nature of women. He believed in the basic goodness of human nature and propagated the ideal of complete man and complete woman, both able to offer unconditional love while working for a common goal.

Gandhi's influence helped women assert their will. It was due to his leadership that women were given rights equal to men in India's Constitution. The history of the women's participation in the freedom struggle in response to Gandhi's call is one of the most fascinating stories of the rise of the Indian female. The Indian women of the late nineteenth century and early twentieth century who had led a life of drudgery behind *purdah* finally emerged free of the web that had held them captive for centuries.

Great reformers like Gandhi drew attention to the goodness inherent in women and made an appeal for an understanding of their human need. Men became aware of the love and affection which women were capable of bestowing. Many women realised that they were not inferior beings and were proud of the key role they played in the survival of human race. An important Muslim reformer of the early twentieth century, Sir Sayyid Ahmad Khan, began a movement for the education of Muslims under the western influence. However, he excluded women from his scheme and firmly opposed their education. In contrast Molvi Nazir Ahmad and Hali were in favour of education of women. Perhaps, because of the influence of his mother on his early life Sir Sayyid saw no need for women's education other than home learning. He opposed starting schools for girls but emphasised the education of Muslim boys at Aligarh.[10] On the other hand, Hali had his women characters reflect on the backward condition of Muslim community, the stagnation of vernacular learning, and the need for girls to be educated in order to fulfil their household and family duties. He did not go to extremes; however, the reforms he advocated were justified in terms of women's traditional role.[11] In a magnificent poem called *Homage to Silence* Hali versified the role of women and their right to education.[12]

Among the foreign women who came to India to serve the cause of women's emancipation, the names of Margaret Noble, later known as Sister Nivedita, Annie Besant and Margaret Cousins stand out. These women of Irish origin and former participants in Irish Home Rule agitation took up the cause of the downtrodden and underprivileged in India.

In 1917 the question of women's franchise was mooted. A deputation of women headed by Sarojini Naidu as spokesperson presented a memorandum to the British Secretary of State in 1919. This deputation demanded women's suffrage as well as increased educational and health facilities. The decision about the franchise was left to the Indian legislatures. With little opposition from these legislatures, thanks to the influence of the reformers, by 1929 women were enfranchised equally with men.[13]

Although women were granted political rights equal to men, much reformative work was still needed to be done as *purdah* and child marriages continued to be the dominant traditions. The laws of inheritance and divorce to assert their will legally restricted women. Illiteracy was predominant and so also the dowry customs. Women's organisations raised these issues for review. Enlightened Congress leaders like Nehru, Patel and Rajendra Prasad gave their full support for removing social and legal inequalities, which had been put upon women. Some of the women leaders who deserve acknowledgement for their efforts in achieving higher status for women in Indian society are chronologically: Annie Besant, Sarojini Naidu, Muthulakshmi Reddi and Raj Kumari Amrit Kaur.

Some interesting events occurred in 1929 when Gandhiji started *Satyagraha,* a freedom movement into which many women entered whole-heartedly. To Mahatma's Dandi march in defiance to the salt law, women gave their full support. Within the next three years of this march, over five thousand women served terms of severe imprisonment, suffered from lathi blows, cruelty, loss of livelihood and ill health. They picketed wine shops and shops that sold foreign clothe. They faced trials in law courts, suffered atrocities in prisons and were defamed for denouncing *purdah* and other evil social customs by the orthodox community leaders. Society came to realise, to some extent, the capacities of women as wilful responsible persons. Men and women began developing mutual respect. The prominent women of this period were neither an enigma nor a myth but were real people fighting for their independence. Sarojini Naidu, Kamla Nehru, Rukmani Lakhshmipathi, Hansa Mehta, Nellie Sen Gupta, Satyavati Devi, Miraben (Ms Slade), Durgabai and Kuttimala Amma all contributed richly to the destruction of the many strands of the web, which had dictated that women were either goddesses or witches. The above mentioned women were compassionate people who worked very hard for the good of all and for the betterment of their country.

In the general elections of February 1939, nearly five million women voters participated enthusiastically in electioneering. The majority of their votes were cast for Congress. It became clear that women could responsibly vote and the doubts of the orthodox men that the enfranchisement of women would bring their country to doom were quickly dispelled. The women who contested on the Congress ticket were extraordinarily successful. In one constituency, a woman elementary school teacher defeated the Vice-Chancellor of the University of her Province. In another, the wife of a doctor overthrew the President of a District Board who had represented the constituency in Parliament for twelve years. In thirty-nine years, India underwent such sweeping changes that by 1939, political, educational and social position for women had risen so high that eight women were members of provincial and state legislatures. India ranked third among the nations of the world in regards to the political influence and position secured by its women. The United States and Russia were first and second respectively.[14]

Viney Kirpal in her introduction to the edited book, *The Girl Child in 20h Century Indian Literature* writes about the depiction of the girl child in the literature of pre-independence period that "as in ancient literature, girl children are not presented as girl children. Their chronological age might place them as children but they appear in those works as "miniature women—child brides, child wives, child widows". The girls may be young in age but the responsibilities they are depicted to be taking up are those of grown up women. She further reports that "the period of adolescence and the transition to womanhood is like a blank page in these texts" [15]

After Independence in 1947, most of the evils in Indian society were vigorously brought to the focus of attention of the nation. The principle of equality among the sexes was effectively put into law. Those ideas were constitutionally accepted by the Indian people who had been prevalent in the advanced nations for a long time. When the Constitution of India was framed in November 1949, its Preamble stated that equality among the sexes was a fundamental right. Many other laws were enacted, intense efforts were made to remove the long-standing legal disabilities around women. It is worth noting that equal voting rights for women were given the very day the Indian Constitution was adopted.

Presently, the government offers incentives to women to enable them to obtain an education that will remove sex discriminations. No woman can now be refused employment because of sex. At present quite a number of women hold jobs in top administrative and managerial services. Almost all the services are open to women who are involved in serious competition with men for the topmost positions in foreign services, police and engineering. They have also found employment in areas such as nuclear engineering, flying and paratroops.

The Hindu Marriage Act of 1955 gave women the legal right to divorce. The daughter who was completely excluded from the inheritance of property among Hindus after the Vedic period now has this right which was granted by The Hindu Succession Act of 1956. In 1961 the Dowry Prohibition Act was passed. The Government began family planning incentive programme as a social welfare measure to release women from unlimited child bearing responsibilities.

In spite of these measures to ensure equality, most women of India are sill tradition bound. Cormack, Rama Mehta, Promilla Kapur, Goldstein and others who have studied the thinking and the outlook of modern Indian women through questionnaire and Interview techniques found that the women, even the highly educated ones, are still completely rooted in their families. The unmarried still depend on their fathers for advice and guidance as well as for the choice of their husbands. The married depend on their husbands for advice about their careers, life-styles and future life plans. These women have identities, which have meaning only in terms of men in their lives. Independence as is found in Western women is lacking in most of Indian women who are willing to sacrifice their independence and identity for the family and for their men who get precedence over their own selves. Since society as a whole accepts this orientation, those who challenge this notion have a difficult time. Divorce is still a hated word in most of the Indian families. Nearly ninety per cent of all marriages among the middle classes are the arranged marriages. The choice of marriage partners depends on the parents.

The education of women is now considered as an essential feature of our national life. The point worth consideration is that: "should education strive to change this situation or strengthen these practices?" Many scholars are of the opinion that the stability of the Indian society is due to the prevalent practices while the exponents of the Women's Liberation Movement are very much against the undermining of women's position in any respect. They want them to be assertive and the determiners of their own destiny. In this connection the views of India's foremost poet, novelist, dramatist and philosopher who expresses them through his heroine Chitra are worth reflecting upon. Chitra speaks out:

> "I am no goddess to be worshipped, not yet the object of common pity to be brushed aside with indifference. Keep me by your side in the path of daring and danger, allow me to share the great duties of your life, then you will know my true self."

REFERENCES

1. S. Shridevi, *A Century of Indian Womanhood*, (Mysore, 1965), pp. 24-25.
2. Shridevi, p. 27.
3. Sangeeta Sharma, "Indian Renaissance, Concept of Womenhood and Dayanand Saraswati" in *Women Images*, (Jaipur, 1996), p. 182.

4. Shridevi, pp. 27-34.
5. Sarasvati Pundita Ramabai. *The High Caste Hindu Woman*, (Philadelphia, 1888), p. 119.
6. M.K. Gandhi, "Young India", in *Women and Social Injustice*, (Ahmedabad, 1942), p. 108.
7. Gandhi, pp. 57, 96, 122.
8. Gandhi, p. 155.
9. A.K. Saxena, "Gandhian Attitude Towards Women's Life," in *The Overseas Hindustan Times*, 5-29-75.
10. Gail Minault, *Secluded Scholars, Women's Education and Muslim Social Reform in Colonial India*, (Delhi, 1998), p. 18.
11. Gail Minault, p. 43.
12. Sakinatul Fatim Wazir Hasan, "Indian Muslim Women. A perspective," in *In our Cause* (Allahabad, 1937), pp. 22-23.
13. Aruna Asaf Ali, Women's suffrage in India," in *In Our Cause*, p. 353.
14. Margaret E. Cousins, "Towards Progress and Freedom" in *The Awakening of Indian Women*, (Madras, 1939), p. 51.
15. Viney Kirpal, *The Girl Child in 20th Century Indian Literature*, (New Delhi, 1992), p. ix.

4

REARING OF GIRL CHILD AND HER EDUCATION

In order to understand the present conditions of rearing and education of girls in India, a review of rearing up practices of the girls in the past is necessary. It may be noted that the girls could remain unmarried until the age of sixteen up to 300 BC. The years before marriage were utilised for education with emphasis on obtaining desirable husbands. To this end girls were given eight or nine years of training. They learned by rote the Vedic hymns prescribed for daily and periodical prayers. Grown up girls were important units in their parents' household. They worked hard and looked after guests. "Music and dancing formed the principal indoor games. Public and dramatic concerts were often organised and girls used to go out to see them along with their elders and lovers".[1] This situation changed after 300 BC. When the new custom of child marriages was introduced. By the beginning of the Christian era, pre-puberty marriages were common. Thus the girls' education suffered since it was difficult to educate them in the short period they were in their parents homes.

During the Muslim period, girls were treated as a curse. The unstable conditions in India made the position of the women very precarious. Whenever a battle was fought and won, the conquerors looted the town as their first reward. Then they took the girls and young women as captives. No young and beautiful girl was safe even during periods of peace because any male possessing force and power could abduct her and make her his concubine, slave or wife depending on his whims. In order to protect the girls they were put behind purdah and married very young. Thus girls experienced the onset of puberty in their husbands' homes, and by the time any tensions were felt due to physiological changes, they were mothers. Hence the Indian girls had no adolescence as we define it today. From childhood, they entered into the adult responsibility of motherhood. This situation made women entirely dependent upon their husbands. They had neither education nor any training for coping with their problems of womanhood. This situation continued into the British period. During the later part of the nineteenth century, many movements emerged which raised the status of women. The reality oriented approaches described earlier, helped parents recognise that their daughters deserved better treatment. By the beginning of the twentieth century attention towards the better rearing practices and education of girls began to be explicitly directed. At the time of India's independence, the need for adequate educational opportunities for girls was widely recognised and the attitude towards daughters in the family underwent a great transformation.

As was pointed out in the previous chapters, women even now are not able to give themselves the total freedom that is theirs for the taking. A tendency still exists to elevate women to the pedestal of goddesses and deny them the right to human successes and failures. This leads to confusion producing state, which is clearly evident in the prevalent practices of the rearing of the girl child. Even after girls are legally independent, they remain fully dependent on their parents. This duality may be explained by four value crises, which may be put in the form of dichotomies as follows:

1. Dependence versus Independence
2. Subordination versus Domination
3. Home versus Job
4. Family versus Self.

Dependence Versus Independence

This dichotomy refers to the identity, which a girl develops while being reared. In India, her identity is one, which has meaning only through parents or her husband. Most girls seem to fail to develop an identity exclusive to their selves. In a deeper sense, this crisis determines whether the girls are reared to take an independent place in society or simply to marry and remain rooted in family. It is a paradox in the Indian situation that while the educated self-professed liberals and leaders support the cause of women's independence, they raise their daughters in such a manner that they remain traditionally dependent. They by and large are very reluctant to allow them any freedom to make a choice of their own life style. In middle class families, particularly, a conflict exists whereby parents wish to prepare their daughters for earning a living and for adding to the family's income, but any contact with a non-relative male is frowned upon. This complete dependence upon parents before marriage for social contacts and life plans is encouraged even while girls are receiving job training or are in employment.

Since girls are not allowed personal decision-making and lack experience in relating with men, even with their co-workers, they find themselves inadequate in skills to maintain a blossoming career. But it may be noted that since they have moved out of their homes they aspire for independence and this creates unsolved crises in their lives. This situation is very much responsible for serious domestic quarrels, which we will discuss in another chapter.

Subordination Versus Domination

The young Indian girl learns the responsibilities of house-keeping and child care quite early in her life. She provides a role model for her younger brothers and sisters. Even a younger daughter is expected to be more responsible than her elder brother who may refuse to do any household work. A young girl is expected to care for and discipline her younger siblings. She is, however, not consulted in any serious family matter. Her opinion on even simple matters is not given much weight. She is expected to command respect from her siblings by her poise, reserve and attitude but at the same time she is given a subordinate place in the family.

This subordination-domination matrix has tremendous influence on the development of the Indian girl's adult personality. She realises that she has to discipline her younger siblings and put over them a dominating influence but at the same time she holds a subordinate position in the household as compared to the male members of the family. This situation creates frustrations. The roots of frustration may be the feelings of helplessness and dependence. Women's outlets for these frustrations range from excessive fasting and fanatic observance to rituals to strict observance of moral codes. We may say that the crises of subordination versus domination leads to the emergence of disciplined daughters, sacrificing mothers and dominant mothers-in law.

Home Versus Job

This crises follows as a corollary of the first crises. If the girls are reared simply for marriage, they need no job oriented education. If they are to have independent status, they must be trained for various vocations. Many people still frown upon job training for women. However, the number of those in favour of working women seems to be increasing because of the economic difficulties. It is being increasingly realised that every adult member in the family must earn. The concept of ideal women now has one dimension more, that is, she serves her husband and family devotedly and also contributes to the economic betterment of the family by taking up a job.

Traditionally, man is the wage earner with woman as the helpmate. But this concept is changing now. The working women are needed for raising the economic standards of the family. Hence girls are being prepared for jobs. But this change is being sought to be brought about without any attempt to compensate or change their roles as housewives and mothers. Thus the expectations and responsibilities which are now being assigned to the women are highly demanding. It is now being expected that the women may look after the homes and also augment the family income, a role subordinate to the male wage earner. This perception of women as a supplementary wage earner conflicts with the idea of women's independent status.

Family Versus Self

This value conflict is rooted in the fact that women have been raised to sacrifice their needs for their families. The validity of this tradition is now being challenged. Women are becoming aware of their rights to develop their own potentials to the fullest. If a woman finds her self crushed under the responsibility and obligation to her family, she may think of revolting against such state of affairs. This raises two issues: should a girl defy her husband or parent if he interferes with her independence? Or should she continue to cling to him even when she is being maltreated?

In order to fully understand the impact of these four value crises on the life of an Indian woman, child rearing practices are needed to be explored. Girls are reared in an environment in which it is often pointed out to them that they are girls and must expect different treatment than that given to the boys. From about five years of age they are taught to do some household jobs. They are also trained to speak slowly and softly and to curb their temper. Any show of aggression is punished in case of girls but in the case of boys it is not only tolerated but also appreciated. Often boys and girls are segregated at an early age. In many modern Indian families even when both boys and girls are given equal affection, the boys get comparatively more privileges by way of freedom of movement outside their homes, etc.

From the age of six to eleven, girls from middle and upper classes are sent to girls' schools or where such schools are not availables than to co-educational schools. The weaker sections of the society do not send girls to schools because they are needed at home to provide domestic help while their mothers are working. Indian girls are by and large not given correct and proper information about menstruation, which many girls experience at fairly early age, maybe between the ages of 10 and 11 years. The girl's mother simply tells her what to do to protect her where her first period occurs. This notion still exists that a menstruating woman is unclean and menstruating girls are not allowed to participate in many activities. Even though silence is maintained while the girl is having her period, the whole family comes to know about it, particularly if some festival or religious ceremony falls during this period in which the girl is not allowed to participate. Recently many opinions have been voiced against this unfair treatment of the menstruating girl. A girl is now expected to compete equally with boys in studies and other activities and for this it is considered essential that no taboos should be put on her during this natural cycle.

Recently the advertisements on television by the manufacturing companies of sanitary napkins are creating awareness of hygienic methods of protection. This, no doubt, is a desirable step but its motive is only to increase the sales of napkins rather than to provide adequate and scientific information.

Margaret Cormack reported in her study of Hindu women that the onset of puberty does not generally produce tension in the girls' lives. The girls do not view puberty as a traumatic period in spite of its surprising onset for which they were not prepared. Her own conclusion is that adolescence for Indian girls is a time of private hurt rather than a time of storm and stress which is so common among American adolescents.[2] Cormack's study was conducted in 1953 when girls were still married fairly young and women had only began to realise their potential freedom. Today, the adolescent girls are becoming increasingly aware of the physical changes and are challenging any restriction on their movements during their menstrual cycle. But there are no overt signs of revolt among Indian adolescent girls. Perhaps they are not courageous enough to openly defy the ages old customs and traditions. Still the enlightened among them are not prepared to accept a subordinate position on the basis of the physiological facts of life. They, however, face insurmountable difficulties because of the attitudes of parents and relatives (both female as well as male). They consider female physiology as their destiny somewhat following Freudian jargon. Even in the modern times often the adolescent girls are pressurised to remain as coy and helpless virgins.

The chances for girls to develop an independent nature are bleak because of their limited social life. They are discouraged from speaking with confidence and self-assurance, even with other women. Parents and other family members ruthlessly curb any assertive attitude or display. Such rearing practices make girls resistant to change and encourage them to cling to the supernatural and superstitions. They begin to believe that their destiny is determined by the gods as inferior individuals in comparison to men and they are born as women because of some sin committed by them in their previous life. This feeling of sin in the past life develops in them an attitude of fatalism. They learn to compromise with the ill-treatment from men.

If a girl falls ill during her childhood she may not receive: as much care as a male child. Lower class illiterate persons leave an ill girl to the mercy of the gods for her cure and care and hardly provide her any medical care. This many be the reason for the lower ratio of females to males in India. According to demographic surveys the females are less in numbers than the males in India. The neglect of the female child also accounts for some personality peculiarities which develop in them. They become docile, meek and sacrificing as well as rigid traditionalists.

At the onset of puberty, girls are strictly supervised and are banned from moving out of their homes all alone particularly after night. Mixing with the boys is totally forbidden except with those who are relatives or well known to the families. They are now being sent to the schools and colleges particularly, those who live in the urban areas and who belong to those classes which are much above the poverty line. The goal of education in most cases remains that of making the girls more marketable in the marriage market. Education often ends when a girl's parents are able to find a suitable mate for her. A wife follows her husband's advice about working after marriage. Brought up in a strict environment as virgins, who have not learnt any decision-making strategies, these girls develop subordinate personalities. The modern girl hears about equality of sexes and empowerment of women but because of her upbringing finds herself helpless in asserting her will. She then broods on her fate and her life suffers from tensions. This leads to marital or familial conflicts for which the girl or woman is considered as the culprit in the male dominated society.

Most girls remain ignorant about sex except whatever information they secretly gather from their classmates or from their peer group. Sex education is not given to the Indian girls and parents are too embarrassed or inhibited to open this issue with their daughters. The psychologists accept that adolescence is the period at which the attitudes towards adult sexuality are established. By and large the adolescent Indian girl is brought up in an environment in which sex not only is considered as secret but immoral. This certainly adversely affects their marital life.

Because of high premium placed on virginity in India pre-marital sex is rare and because of the taboo put on extra-marital sex with other males, the woman's husband is her sole source of pleasure. While no taboos are placed on conjugal sex, the wife usually assumes a passive role in sex act. Any initiative by wife for sex is interpreted in terms of her being immoral or corrupt. But this was not the case in early Indian tradition. The women in ancient India were not so docile in sex matters. In many temples the outer walls have life-size murals showing every imaginable pose for intercourse. The temples at Khajurao are the testimony of this observation. These temples are still used, as are many others, and the deities in them are still worshipped. The paintings in the Ajanta caves and the sculptures in Ellora caves are full of vigour and life.

It may also be noted that the young Indian girls in devout Hindu family sing songs, which describe the love affairs of the celestial beings that even describe explicit erotic activities. The girls are taught that their husbands are to be treated as gods. Thus in their minds it is ingrained that they must submit completely to the wishes of their husbands even in the matters of sex. They are reared in such a fashion that they cannot think of anything else besides complete devotion to their husbands. They learn to wait patiently for their husbands to take them in whatever manner they like in the sex act, just as a devotee of god awaits the god's pleasure.

In modern India changes in this type of mentality are taking place. The impact of education and the exposure to the other cultures is bringing a tremendous change in the attitudes of the Indian girls. The social milieu is changing. The women have become conscious of their rights. They are now learning to challenge the authority of the males. The society is in transition. However, the transitional society, which now exists in India, is posing problems to the rearing of girls because of the four value crises, which we have discussed above. The parents do not know whether to continue to cling to the traditions in rearing the girls or move towards modernism by training their daughters towards equality of sexes and independence of outlook. In order to help the parents to solve the problem of status quo versus modernity a comprehensive scheme of parental education is needed. This scheme may emphasise the modern outlook but may still keep the Indian cultural values intact.

According to a report of the "National Committee on the Status of Women in India (1971-74)," the vast majority of Indian women were still ignorant. One-third of the total population of girls never went to school and only 30 per cent of those who attended school attained functional literacy. Even though more than 25 years have passed since this report was published it may be asserted that the situation has not improved much. No doubt the number of schools and the number of girls attending them have increased manifold but the growth of population had undermined all the efforts in very greatly improving the percentage of girls to the total population of girls of school going-age, attending the schools.

The men and women of the lower classes are so busy in earning a living and surviving that the children of these classes have to undertake adult responsibilities at a very early age. They become wage earners or domestic helpers and have no time or inclination to attend school. Among the lower middle classes education of the girls is favoured and considered a social and economic need but many girls have to drop out from schools because of the parent's poor financial state. The double expenditure of educating a daughter and then providing dowry at the time of her marriage deters many parents from continuing with educational expenses.

There is an imperative need in this country of educating the women. Women of all ages benefit from education. The mothers have tremendous influence on the attitudes and aspirations of their daughters. In case they are illiterate and superstitious they exercise unhealthy influence on their daughters. It is only through education that the new generations' ties with conservatism may possibly be broken. The education of mothers is essential for developing an enlightened nation.

A medium, which has become very powerful in influencing the attitudes, ideals and the values of the women, is television. Unfortunately, this medium has not been fully exploited so far for bringing the desirable attitudinal changes in the outlook of our female population. The serials on this medium are mostly showing either ultra modern life or offer the absurd superstitious episodes. Both sides are harmful for the development of a balanced personality. Films, which portray an uneducated, docile, subservient wife who worships her husband as an ideal of womanhood, convey the wrong message that the woman's salvation lies only in being an obedient wife and leading a life of subordination. Women learn from these films that they must suffer their indignities silently and wait for God's intervention for the mitigation of their sufferings. The psychological damage, which such films, serials or episodes cause to the selves of the young girls and the women, is very detrimental to the status and the position of the women.

It may be said that for centuries the women have been trapped in a mythical web of subordination by such tactics which have involved stories, dramas, tales, fables, discourses, songs, poems and episodes. In the present times the more powerful media are available to focus on such myth. Education is needed to undermine the negative influence of such media and to exploit these for creating an awareness of equality of sexes and the true meaning and potential of feminism.

REFERENCES

1. A.S. Alterkar, *The Position of Women in Hindu Civilization*. (Delhi, 1962), p.15.
2. Margaret Cormack. *The Hindu Woman*, (New York, 1953), pp.79-80.
3. Ashish Bose, A Demographic Profile of Indian Women in *Indian Women*, (New Delhi, 1975), p.141.

5

FEMALE PSYCHE AND MARITAL RELATION

The Indian woman's life revolves around her dual roles of wife and mother. She lives to serve her husband and to give birth to his children. Her upbringing, activities and aspirations are all tied to these two roles. Therefore, the marriage is her major goal and purpose in her life. Since she desires children, sex is necessary, but her own enjoyment is secondary to that of her husband. She may enjoy sex but any overt expression of this enjoyment is unacceptable. She is faithful to her husband and serves him with her body, mind and spirit. Pre-marital, extra-marital and sex after widowhood are despised and disapproved by the society.

Love to the Indian woman means self-denial and sacrifice for her husband and children. She seldom reflects on her own needs or interests. She merges herself so completely in her dual roles as extensions of her husband and children that she exists as a body without a soul, without a "being" aspect. The Indian culture has propagated this unselfish ideal. However, the points worth pondering over are: Do women really enjoy self-denial? Does the Indian culture really desire that women should be simply the mothers with no individuality of their own? Are women only suited for these two roles of wife and mother? A "yes" response to all these questions may come because of centuries of socialisation, which has controlled the fabric of women's lives. But in case we take the outlook of the modern women into consideration the answer to all these questions would be a clear-cut "no".

Marriage among Hindus is a sacrament and is expected to last whole of the lifetime of the couple. Most of the women belonging to the middle and upper classes live up to this ideal. Among the lower classes where marriage traditionally has not been considered so tie-binding mores are changing. A tendency towards more permanency in marriage is being observed. Generally lower class women are more liberated concerning marriage and divorce customs even though they are often victims of act of sadism committed by their husbands and other males.

Although the two descent systems in India, i.e., matrilineal and patrilineal, differ in some respects, men have recognised authority over women in both the systems. In the matrilineal system, the power rests with the men in wife's family. Men have authority but the lineage is counted through women. A husband does not become a member of his wife's family and his rights over his wife and children are minimal. The wife's brothers, father or uncles control property. Even though the women enjoy more rights and privileges than in the patrilineal system men still make the major decisions regarding her life. The current changes in society are affecting the matrilineal system because men who move from their homes to other parts of the country take their wives and children with them and they, therefore, exercise more power over them. New legislation on marriage, inheritance and dowries is also making this system as redundant.

The majority of the Indian population is patrilineal in its mode of descent. The male is the perpetuator of the lineage and family name. The daughter in this system is ordained to belong to her husband's family rather than the one in which she was born. In either her own or her husband's family, she is subordinate and gains recognition only through her father or husband. Marriage is a religious rite, and the girl's father has a duty to find a husband for her. Among Hindus marriage is performed by the Vedic rites.In other religious groups, it is conducted according to the marriage rites of those religions. Marriages are also performed by civil code. In civil marriages, very small amount of money is spent and the ceremony is very simple. In religious ceremonies, money is lavishly spent and the festivities last for a whole day or for a number of days.

In Hindu marriages, the symbol of union is seven steps taken by the couple around the sacrificial fire in the presence of the priest who at the same time chants the sacred verses. The Hindus have classified marriage into eight types. Each kind is different from the others on the basis of the ceremonies performed. Only four of the eight are approved, and one, the Brahma, is most widely accepted by the upper classes. Most of the high caste Hindus offer dowries to their daughters' husbands at the time of marriage. Many Muslims and Christians of India have adopted this custom but it is not universally acceptable and is considered as an evil by majority of them. The dowry may be labelled as a form of bridegroom purchase.

Whatever might have been the origin of the dowry system in India, it has now become a social evil. The Dowry Act of 1961 failed to introduce any worthwhile measures for the abolition of this evil. Various State Governments have enacted stricter legislation for penalising those that give or receive dowries. The Indian Penal Code makes this practice a penal offense. The social reformers try their best to discourage parents of the girls to offer any dowry. The mass media also makes efforts to shape public opinion against this evil custom. In spite of all these efforts the dowry system has taken so firm roots in the social milieu that it is still a widely prevalent practice.

One of the reasons for the prevalence of the dowry system is the greed of the parents of the bridegroom. They know that the girl's parents are keen to marry her at the earliest and so they demand their price. A spinster in the Indian society is looked down upon. The parents of every girl want that their daughter may get a suitable husband as soon as she is of marriageable age. When the girl is of marriageable age and they select an eligible mate for her they try to fulfil the monetary and other demands of the boy's parents. In choosing the husband for their daughter the parents confine their search to their own caste and religious groups. Mostly their choice of a suitable match for their daughter is confined to a very small segment of their community. Since the choice is limited and the number of eligible bachelors for their daughters is quite limited their is usually a competition among the parents of the girls in roping the boy into matrimony with their daughters. The dowry is the bait, which the parents throw. Because of such conditions existing in the marriage market the abolition of the dowry system has become extremely difficult. The only remedy lies in educating our girls so that they achieve economic independence and assert their free will. They should no more remain a liability for their parents.

The desire for a male child is very deep-rooted in the psyche of Indian people. Pinkham quotes an ancient text in the following words: "Vouchsafe blessings upon the wombs that bring male children forth".[1] The Hindu religious literature also stresses this aspect. The literature emphasises that the couple should be in the proper frame of mind for sexual union in order to produce male offspring. Certain ceremonies are prescribed for the couple before the sexual intercourse. The couple is to dispel all lascivious thoughts and animal desires. The husband and wife both are asked to consciously and deliberately will that progeny shall be spiritual and preferably male. Sex is not considered to be an enjoyable passionate experience. Sexual act is to be performed only for the purpose of propagation. Since the parents in India live with the son, preferential treatment to the son is a normal practice. The economic factor is the main motivation for the aspiration to bear sons. This factor is interwoven with the religious faith that the male and female both believe that for them there is no salvation unless they produce sons in legitimate wedlock.

In spite of the religious downplaying of sex for enjoyment, various erotic texts like the *Kama Sutra* of Vatsyana or Pandit Koka's *Rangmala* and paintings and sculptures on temple walls express sexual interest and enjoyment for its own sake rather than for producing offspring. But this open display of sexual act on the walls of the temples, etc. does not mean that sexual act was an open affair in India at any time of her history. Sexual intercourse has always been a very private affair in India. Recently, however, some studies have indicated that Indian women are expressing an interest in sensitive sex. Promilla Kapur found in her study of the "working women" that sexual maladjustment, irrespective of whether it was the cause or effect of sexual dissatisfaction, was found to be present in nearly ninety-five per cent of the cases of marital maladjusted working women.[2] Many of these women described their husbands as rude, sexually impotent or very direct or brutal in their sexual act. In some cases women reported being turned off sexually when the husband spoke obscenities during sex. Marital adjusted women made no mention of vulgar language. It seems that women do not like being coarsely handled and wanted their husband to treat them with consideration during sexual act.

The practice of child marriages also inhibits the women's sexual responses. In spite of laws against such marriages, they still are prevalent particularly in Rajasthan, Haryana and some other backward states. The origin of child marriages is traced to a myth woven around a Vedic mantra. According to this mantra, the husband says to his bride:

"First, Soma had thee; Gandharva had the next; Agni became thy third lord; the fourth (lord) is I, born of man. Soma gave thee to the Gandharva; the Gandharva gave thee to Agni; then thee to me has Agni given with the capacity to bring forth wealth and progeny".[3]

This led to the belief that it would be the best to marry a girl before Soma and the other gods have enjoyed her. Recent legislation along with better enforcement has reduced the molestation of the adolescent girls and the number of child marriages. Hate's survey published in 1969 had reported that nearly one-fifth of the girls in the age group from ten to fourteen were married.[4] Many of these girls were from rural areas. Since the rural areas are still tradition-bound the situation regarding child marriages might have only marginally changed for the better. According to the survey the average age of marriage in the urban areas was twenty-three. Hate felt that the considerations of caste, status and dowry were the obstacles, which were being overcome as the marriage age was rising.

Since the parents arrange most marriages the mutual physical attraction which is an important aspect of sexual enjoyment does not form the criterion for making the choice of the life partner. Arranged marriages have many features, which highlight the unequal status of women with men. A very common practice is that the girl is presented before the boy with whom there is a proposal of her marriage. She is shown as a commodity, which is being sold in the market. The psychological impact on the girl of such a practice is usually very bad especially when the boy or his parents reject her. Some girls who are rejected again and again suffer severe mental tensions so much so that they either commit suicide or reach up to the stage of taking such an extreme step.

The marriage contracts of the Muslims give unequal rights to the men and women. It permits unilateral right of divorce and polygamy to the husband. The bride's consent to marriage is a mere formality. The institution of marriage places her in a subordinate position. Muslim women get some security against the possibility of divorce by Mehar (dower), but very few women are able to assert this claim. While Islam recognises women's right to inherit property, in practice this right is rarely upheld. The Muslim man can divorce his wife at any time with only an obligation to pay the dower, a sum fixed at the time of marriage. The Muslim woman is, however, free to remarry as soon as her period of *Iddat* is over. This period of *Iddat* is prescribed to avoid confusion over parentage in case of pregnancy.

In Hate's study Muslim maidens were asked if they would put down any conditions for marriage. All replied that they had no say at all in the choice of mate or marriage arrangements which were all taken care of by the elders.[5] When Margaret Cormack questioned Indian informants who were female graduate students at Columbia University, she was told that they were surprised that the Western marriage vows use the word "Obey". They disapprove the legal enforcement of obedience. This might be due to their exposure to the freedom enjoyed by the women in the United States at that time and to the movements for women liberation at the time of the study conducted by Cormack. Abolishing of such a vow would be unthinkable in a Hindu marriage ceremony.[6] Obedience to husbands is part of the socialisation process in India and needs no legal reinforcement.

In the opinion of Jamila Brij Bhushan "Muslim women can have a position of economic and personal independence that could be the envy of women in all but the most liberal countries." She believes that the Muslim women do not exercise their rights in India. She opines that "Call it masochism, call it the culture or whatever you like but the fact remains that the majority of them will not reach out to grasp something that is theirs by right and can, under no circumstances be denied to them".[7] No doubt the Muslim women in India are as weak-willed as other women belonging to other religious groups. They are just as dependent upon their men for guidance and support as others. Modesty, decorum and chastity are the virtues that are inculcated in them since early childhood. Muslim law has at least endeavoured to provide economic security to women for whole of their lives but the women largely ignore these provisions. In those cases where the women take initiative to assert their rights the male ego comes forward to interpret the law in such a manner that the women are further humiliated. Jamila observes that "no respectable woman would dream of claiming her dower money".[8]

Muslim la considers marriage as a contract but in modern Muslim life, especially among the higher echelon of society, it is considered as sacrosanct for women. This may be due to the cultural configuration as well as the

Muslim male's urge to dominate and usurp many rights of the women so that they remain dependent and ignorant. The main reason for placing men in authority over women, however, is the frequently cited verse in the holy Quran:

"Men are the managers of the affairs of women,
For that God has preferred in bounty
One of them over another, and for that
They have expanded of their property
Righteous women are therefore obedient...[9].

Gail Minaulet writes:

"In the matter of court witness, where two women's testimony equal to that of one man, Mumtaz Ali points out that the verse in Quoran refers specifically to business matters, in which women may have less experience. But their lack of experience is a product of social conditions, not an inherent defect."[10]

Among Christians, the biblical image of woman as temptress and seductress has strengthened the husband's right to control his wife and her property. Even though the taboos on women's freedom are less evident among Christians, women are considered subordinate to men. Among Christians incest, adultery, bigamy with adultery, rape, sodomy, bestiality, or the husband's apostasy from Christianity coupled with marriage to another woman all give the wife the grounds for divorce. But according to this religion, "women is the unclean one, the seducer, who brought sin into the world and caused the fall of man. Consequently all apostles and fathers of Church have regarded marriage as an inevitable evil, just as prostitution is regarded today"[11]. Peter tells women emphatically: "Be obedient unto your husbands"[12]. Paul also raises his influential voice against the higher education and culture of women, when he says:

"Let the woman learn in silence with all subjection, but I suffer not a woman to teach, nor to usurp authority over the man, but to bear in silence"[13].

Augest Bebel emphasises.

"At the creation woman is commanded to be subject unto man. The ten commandments of the Old Testament are as a matter of fact addressed only to man, for the tenth commandment names woman along with the servant and the domestic animals. In truth, woman was a piece of property, which man obtained for a price for a corresponding service on his part"[14].

Raman Lal Mehta wrote in 1933 that the failure of marriages in Hindu society was a comment on the sacred concept of these marriages. The woman was forced to submit to her husband's every whim and to calmly endure crude habits without any recourse to dissolve the union. He believed that in itself was enough to call for an immediate change in the Hindu system and marriage concept[15].

The Marriage Act of 1955 introduced a number of reforms in Hindu women's legal rights. It disallows bigamy, which is punishable as a crime. Relief by way of judicial separation, declaration of nullity of marriage and divorce are permissible under this Act. It permits women divorce on the grounds of adultery, change in religion, insanity, leprosy or venereal disease, renouncement of the world to become ascetic and desertion for seven years. Divorce is also allowed if their husbands are guilty of rape, sodomy, or bestiality. Desertion and cruelty are grounds for legal separation and eventual divorce if continued over a long period of time.

The Special Marriage Act of 1954 gave sanction to people of different faith to marry each other. Any male over twenty-one years and any female over eighteen years can marry under the provisions of this Act. This form of marriage can also be dissolved by divorce.

Another Act which has helped provide equality is the Hindu Succession Act of 1956. Previously a Hindu woman could not own any other property except her *streedharan* or those valuables offered to her at the time of her marriage. According to this Act the widow and mother are now entitled to inherit the property of the deceased husband or son.

Hindu women now have the right to hold, sell, mortgage or donate property if they so wish.

Two other Acts have also greatly helped the women. The Hindu Adoption and Maintenance Act of 1956 allow a son or daughter for adoption by the husband with the consent of the wife. Previously, there was no provision for adoption of the daughter. A wife is also allowed to claim maintenance even if she is living separately from her husband, provided he is proved to be a guilty party. The Medical Termination of Pregnancy Act of 1971 aimed to reduce the incidence of criminal abortions. This Act allows termination of pregnancy on therapeutic grounds, eugenic grounds, humanitarian grounds or social grounds.

These and some other recent legislations have been enacted in an attempt to allow women to attain higher status and equality of rights with men. Many other measures have also been taken to give women a place of dignity in the society. They are in the process of being given 30 per cent reservations in the Parliament and State Assemblies and also in the Government jobs. But unfortunately these laws and measures have little meaning to the majority of Indian women. The main reasons for this state of affairs are two overlapping factors. The majority of women, belonging to the poorer and backward sections of the society are illiterate and ignorant, and secondly, the myths woven around their obligations for serving their male relations are much more powerful than any law or reformists words.

In our country widows outnumber widowers about four to one who have not remarried. This indicates that deterrents to remarriage of widows are still highly activated in spite of the Hindu Widows Remarriage Act, 1956 that legalised the remarriage of Hindu widows. One major reason for this state of affairs seems to be the absence of a mass movement by the women to achieve their legal and human rights. The high-class society women mostly dominate the women organisations, which are working in the direction of empowerment of the women. Their efforts are confined to the educated women only. Their impact on the rural or slum area women is almost negligible so also on the orthodox and traditionally oriented women. The male members also look their efforts with suspicion. It may be this factor that the reservation bill in our Parliament is finding much opposition from a section of the parliamentarians who are asking for the reservations within 30 per cent for the women of the minority communities and backward classes.

Why have the majority of the Indian women not revolted against the tyranny of centuries of subordination? Pondering over this question gives an interesting insight into the psyche of the Indian women. In the next chapter, the Indian woman's motivations and aspirations are being discussed in an attempt to find out an answer to this question. The educated women are also not very clear about their roles in the households. They wish to assert their independence but do not have much courage to do so because they are afraid of the social sanctions. They typify a real predicament. They desire to be more liberal but when the problem of training of their own daughters comes up they become quite conservative. They wish to inculcate such values in their daughters as self-sacrifice, self-effacement, modesty and reserve and when daughters do not accept these values they are very much agitated. These women know that the old values are difficult to inculcate but they are also not prepared to accept the new values that are based on the modern western values of complete liberalisation.

This dilemma is universal in India today. The parents are in confusion. They continue to idealise Indian traditions that they know cannot continue to exist. The younger generation drifts because of this indecision on the part of their parents. The task of education then becomes to steer a clear path out of the confusion between the old and new. The present generation can neither ignore the Indian ideals nor can remain completely insulated from the modern outlook which emphasises the women's complete freedom of will and action. What is best for the Indian girls must be propagated by the Indian educational system. The educationists must try to evolve out from the good ideals prevalent in India for centuries the modern outlook. This means that the Indian girls should have freedom of will but do not turn away from their domestic duties. They must learn to understand that absolute freedom is neither feasible nor desirable but a life of subordination and denial of will is also not to be tolerated.

REFERENCES

1. Mildreth Worth Pinkham, *Women in the Sacred Scripture of Hinduism*, (New York, 1967), p. 24.
2. Promila Kapur, *Marriage and the Working Women in India*, (Delhi, 1975), p. 420
3. P. Thomas, *Women and Marriage in India*, (London, 1939), p. 95.
4. Chandrakala Hate, *Changing Status of Women in Post-independence India*, (Bombay, 1969).
5. Hate, p. 38.
6. Margaret Cormack, *The Hindu Women*, (New York, 1953), p. 128.
7. Jamila Brij Bhushan, "The Unassertive Sex" in *The Hindustan Times* Weekly (1-11-76).
8. Jamila Brij Bhushan, In *The Hindustan Times* Weekly.
9. A.J. Arberry, *The Koran Interpreted*. 1, p. 105.
10. Gaul Minaulet, *Secluded Scholars, Women's Education and Muslim Social Reform in Colonial India*, (Delhi, 1998), p. 80.
11. Subrata, Mukerjee and Sushila Ramaswami (ed.). August Bebel, *Women in the Past, Present and Future*, (New Delhi, 1996), p. 22.
12. Mukerjee and Ramaswami, p. 23.
13. *Ibid.*, p. 23.
14. *Ibid.*, p. 21.
15. Raman Lal Mehta quoted in Chandra Kala Hate. *Hindu Women and Her Future*, (Bombay, 1948).

6

ASPIRATIONS AND MOTIVATIONS OF INDIAN WOMEN

The Webster's New World Dictionary of the American language defines aspirations as "strange desire or ambition, as for advancement?" What are the ambitions of the Indian women? What are their desires? What do they consider as advancement? How do they strive to fulfil their ambitions?

Motivation can be viewed as one class of determinants of behaviour. What motivates the Indian woman? Her behaviour may give the key to this question. Since psychological determinants cannot be completely isolated from biological, cultural and situational factors, these factors must be taken into consideration while analysing her behaviour pattern of the Indian women. Thus Indian feminine behaviour is the chief concern with motivation as its determinant, and aspirations a secondary factor, which influence both but is not so easily observed.

Both Indian men and women believe that females are the weaker, sex—weaker physically, emotionally and in the opinion of some intellectually as well. Most parents do not want girls because they are considered liabilities. They must be protected, given a dowry and married in a good family. Hence during childhood girls hold an inferior position in the family. The differential treatment they receive develop within them the typical qualities or characteristics of Indian womanhood. The Indian girls upbringing determines their aspirations and motivations. They desire a virtuous, modest life centered around their husbands and children. They aspire for men of good character and education who can maintain them decently as their husbands. In a study by Cora Vreeda de Stuers, girls responded that their parents educated them so that they would be able to marry well.[1] Girls by and large drop out of school as soon as their marriages are arranged unless their betrothed or in-laws wish them to continue their studies. In such cases they continue studies to fulfil the aspirations of others, rather than their own. To another question of Cora put to 203 postgraduate women students of Jaipur the answers were on traditional lines. The women reported that: "a woman's main destiny to be is marriage and motherhood."[2]

The themes of the popular films, modern novels, love songs and other works of art all portray the Indian girl as a modest, shy, beautiful and delicate being who often dreams of a prince charming rather than a career. The aspirations of a woman after her marriage are confined to her family's welfare and needs. Even working married women are more concerned about their families than their jobs. If a conflict occurs, the family comes first. They welcome pregnancy as a chance to bear a male child. Cora wrote that "the girls had difficulty in imagining their married lives other than in serving their husbands and the children they would bear them."[3]

Why is the Indian woman so rooted in her family? It may be said that it is centuries of socialisation, which has shaped her behaviour. Modern Indian writers point out that women of Vedic times had high status, but her position has degenerated since then. However, in the Vedic times also the woman's husband and offspring were her major concern. This may be attributed to the division of labour, which the society had approved in the very begining of civilisation. Women were given the task of tending the homes and men the fields and arms. This division of labour was further made rigid when women were put behind *purdah* and men became absolute lords of their lives. Till recently the Indian woman was not allowed the opportunity to expand her horizons. Unfortunately even today very few models exist to show her how to develop her personality beyond the home environment.

Two studies done in sixties and seventies indicated a changing trend regarding the motivation for marriage. Kapur's two-phase, ten-year study found that women in the sixties married for social, economic or emotional security. In the seventies they responded that mutual companionship and satisfaction of needs were as important considerations as the earlier ones.[4] At the beginning of twentyfirst century the motivations for marriage may still be in the direction of personal satisfaction and mutual companionship. The security aspect may further be undermined because the women of the middle classes are joining the world of work in larger numbers and the enrollment of girls in higher education is increasing very rapidly and not only this the women are excelling in all the fields of work may it be Army or Police.

Another study by Barot reported in 1972 also revealed that the women's attitudes towards marriage had undergone change in that the emphasis had shifted from self-sacrifice to personal and mutual satisfaction.[5] Unfortunately the shift was more towards obtaining material comforts from marriage rather than affection and love. Some women might be cold and calculating in weighing the advantages of marriage. In sixties and seventies quite a large number of arranged marriages were taking place. Merchant examined some statistic regarding this practice. He found that in 1935, 78 per cent of the respondents favoured marriage by their choice.[6] Hate found that in 1946, 74 per cent of her unmarried respondents wished to choose their own partner's.[7] Kapur's 1959 study revealed that only 48 per cent preferred marriage based on love.[8] Other studies by Jauhari, Mehta and Cormack during decades up to seventies also show the trend towards the liking of arranged marriages. All these studies had educated women as respondents, therefore, it may be concluded that the Indian women of these decades wanted the best of both the worlds—mutual acceptance, material comforts and parental approval. Kapur called it as a quasi-traditional type of marriage.[9] This might be due to the transitional phase. But it may be seen that even now towards the end of nineties the preference for arranged marriages has not very significantly changed in spite of the girls becoming more assertive in exercising their choice in the selection of their life partners.

Women in the 40's and 50's were full of romanticism born of struggles for emancipation. They envisioned a society where men and women might mix freely socially and make choices based on love. In reality such choices were hard to come by. Women had to either depend on the choice of their parents or remain unmarried. Two other aspects that have affected this situation were the legal granting of equality which conflicted with the ideal as presented by the mass media and tradition. Even among the educated women very few worked to fulfil personal ambition or married for love. Second, very few career women had aspirations to reach to the top level of their profession if it involved in any way the interference with their normal domestic life. Jauhari found in her study that a majority of working women in her sample neither took their work seriously nor had developed any notion of a career.[10]

In a study by Arora, Bhattacharaya and others, which sampled unmarried typists, clerks, stenographers and telephone operators in Bombay, it was found that 60 per cent of the respondents worked only as a stopgap measure until marriage. Only 22 per cent had aspirations for higher official status. The rest expected to simply continue what they were doing without advancement or wished to quit soon and 48 per cent were in favour of employment because of the possibility that it would improve their prospects for marriage. According to this study no one wanted to be just a career woman.[11]

The Indian woman's subordination of her aspirations to the good of her husband and children may indicate a tendency to masochism. Could it be that Indian men are more sadist and Indian women more masochistic than non-Indians are? The *Sati* system does support this supposition. The Brahman priests who tabooed killing of animals were not in the least perturbed when a woman's husband died and she was burnt alive. Some widows burned themselves with pomp and grandeur. This tendency still persists in some men and women as the *sati* ceremony of Roop Kanwar in Rajasthan in the late eighties show. There were people who not only witnessed the gruesome happening but also positively supported the cult of *sati*. This was a clear example of sadism of men and masochism of women.

The abolition of the *sati* system by law in the nineteenth century did not ameliorate the conditions of the Hindu widows. In 1939 Chattopadhayya observed: "Truly as some are reminded that the widow was lifted from the pyre but left in the cremation ground.[12] Certainly in 2000 AD they are out of the cremation ground but are still moving in their own funeral procession with colourless dresses, frugal meals, toil and tears. While compassionless men praise this simplicity they seem to feel a strange masochistic honour in living in such a lifestyle.

In Sengupta's book *The Story of Women in India*, this masochistic tendency is explored. When she asked a woman how she accounted for this accepting, deterministic view of life, the woman replied, "We have this serenity because our sense of duty is so highly developed, our duty towards God, towards our parents, towards husband and children. We think of ourselves last.... And if we meet with misfortune, it is because of our Karma".[13] Sengupta offers this comment, "So it may, for it is bound to make one's lie limited to a narrow area—merely for the lack of ambitions... An Indian woman's ambitions are not so much her own, but her husband's and children's and many an unobtrusive woman has given great men to the world".[14]

Unfortunately, somewhat deeper probing of the psyche of an average Indian woman uncovers a weak willed individual who leaves all decision making up to the man in her life. This woman is afraid to develop her own personality for the fear of offending her husband. From this perspective, it would also follow that such a dedicated woman may aspire to die before or with her husband. Her entire motivation to live is for her husband. It may be mentioned that the Indian women have suffered from mental slavery for centuries. Their indecision, unassertiveness and lack of will have been branded as emerging out of their Karma. These women live every moment of their lives in the blind faith in the theory of Karma. In fact they do not know or do not want to know the true meaning of Karma, which cannot be interpreted in terms of inaction as these women depict in their lifestyle.

The literature in most of the Indian languages propagates the ideal of silent, suffering women. Surrender and self-sacrifice are associated with the personality of the woman. For the housewife the ideal of Sita and Savitri is eulogised. The ideal of *Shakti* is not so frequently emphasised as that of suffering woman. This may be because the power in woman is less acceptable than her humility.

Whatever we have discussed above about the Indian women's psyche may not be very true. Is the Indian woman psychologically a weak creature? So far we have portrayed her as such. But the question raised herein needs much deeper and thorough probe. The Indian woman's psyche has become outwardly as depicted above due to the sociological factors operating in our land for centuries. What is her true nature and what she can become if there are brought about vital changes in our social environment? We will be seized with these questions in the next three chapters of the present book. It may, however, be mentioned here that the modern literature in India as well as the mass media is no more presenting the woman as a weak willed individual.

The modern man in India wants equality between the sexes; in principle. But he feels much difficulty and pain in accepting equality with his wife, daughter, mother or sister. The women demand protection and security from him and in return for it he demands their loyalty and respect. The psyche of modern male seems to be that the women be given their freedom to the extent that they respect his wishes, look after him well and remain loyal and faithful to him. The male wants women to have aspirations as long as they do not come in conflict with his own ambitions. He may allow his wife to move out of the house or join the world of work but he is extremely jealous if she associates with any colleague or friend. On the other hand he feels as his right as a male to mingle with her female colleagues and co-workers. Thus he believes in the double standards of conduct for males and females. The significant difference between the modern Indian male and his ancestors is that he does acknowledge that women have the right to an equal and decent life but it must be lived under his supervision and protection. The modern Indian women do not suffer from as many indignities as the women used to suffer in the past. Still it is desirable that they aspire to be more than mere appendages of their husbands. They should seek a partnership relationship in which the question of superiority and inferiority does not arise nor does one individual engulf the individuality of the other. When a clash of opinion occurs it should be resolved through mutual love, respect and consideration.

The doctrine of *Karma*, which preaches action, is really one of inaction so far as it concerns Indian women. The women are made inert and dependent upon a husband they worship, even if he is unworthy or a parasite on society or is a criminal. This is not what Lord Krishna taught when he motivated Arjuna to fight. Much of the teachings of *Gita* have been twisted in a degenerative social system of the Indian orthodox family.

Spratt provides a psychological reason for this inaction among males as well as females. He believes that the Hindu culture is essentially narcissistic in the Freudian sense. Moddie agrees with him and describes the social consequences of this distinctive Hindu personali y. Spratt stated that a greater gap between aspiration and achievement exists in Indian culture than in most others, but it causes less stress. Hindus are comfortable with this ambivalence and their narcissistic personalities lead to withdrawal from public affairs by some of the most desirable people. This disastrous effect extracts a high price from Indian society.[15]

The Indian female must strive to understand this aspect off her culture. Highly narcissistic attitudes lead to inaction in the face of frustration. In order to keep their mental balance in a society where woman's whole life revolves around her husband woman becomes totally inert when widowed. But this is quite an undesirable situation. Even after her husband's death woman can do much. She must rise above her frustrations and turn inaction into action. She may remarry or she may devote herself to social or national service. Many modern women are doing so but a vast majority of illiterate and semi-educated women fall prey to inaction or to a life of drudgery and toil. The worst aspect of the life of the widows one can see at the religion oriented towns of Varanasi or Brindaban. The relatives of the widows leave them in these towns, as they do not want to support them financially. Having no means of subsistence these widows in order to maintain themselves have no option but to beg and live in extremely inhuman conditions.

The education for the women must be so organised that there occurs a directional change in their aspirations. More avenues of employment must be opened for the women. Special vocational training centres should be established for the widows and the destitute women. The women must be encouraged through a vibrant educational system to be more self-oriented. No doubt such an orientation may lead a new form of frustrations but a good educational system may convert these frustrations as the basis of higher achievements in all walks of life. The danger of frustrations resulting in greater introversion is always present but this can be overcome by the cultivation of a positive and outward outlook towards life.

At present there are various agencies which are working in the direction of woman's empowerment. Their impact is certainly towards the achievement of higher status and position of the women in the society but mostly this impact is being felt in the case of the women belonging to the affluent sections of the society. The women belonging to the poor families or of rural areas are beyond their influence. It is, therefore, extremely desirable that educational effort be extended to these neglected sections of the womanhood. In providing education to them care has to be taken that it develops in them right attitudes, higher aspirations and motivations for better achievements. The education should equip the women for building a better world in which mutual love, respect and effort become the ideals for living.

REFERENCES

1. Cora Vreede de Stuers, *Girl Students in Jaipur, A Study in Attitude Towards Family Life, Marriage and Career,* (N.Y., 970), p. 115.
2. Vreede de Stuers, p. 91.
3. *Ibid.*, p. 91.
4. Promilla Kapur, *The Changing Status of the Working Woman in India,* (Delhi, 1974), p. 10.
5. Jyoti Barot, "Modern Trends in Marital Relations," *The Indian Family in the Change and Challenge of Seventies,* (New Delhi, 1972).
6. K.T. Merchant, *Changing Views on Marriage and Family,* (Madras, 1935).
7. C.A. Hate. "The Social Position of Hindu Women," *Unpublished Ph.D. Thesis,* (Bombay, 1946).
8. Kapur, p. 11.
9. Ibid., p. 12.
10. Prema Jauhari, "Status of Working Women," *Ph.D. Thesis,* (Lucknow, 1970).
11. K.K. Arora, *et.al,* "Women and Career," *Group Project Report* Submitted to the Tata Institute of Social Sciences for Post-graduate Diploma in Social Science Administration with Specialization in Family and Child Welfare, (Bombay, 1963).

12. Kamala Devi Chattapadhay, *et. al, The Awakening of Indian Women,* (Madras, 1939), p. 230.
13. Padamini Sengupta, *The Story of Women in India,* (New Delhi, 1974), p. 230.
14. Sengupta, p. 230.
15. A.D. Moddie, *The Brahmanical Culture and Modernity,* (London, 1968), pp. 78-77.

7

PHYSIOLOGICAL DETERMINANTS OF WOMEN EDUCATION

Are women different from men because of their physiological development? This question is raised time and again. The men establish their superiority by pointing out the biology of the female sex. Whenever the question of the equality of sexes is put someone is sure to say: "But it's just a matter of biology. You know women are different from men—they are more intuitive, nurturing, emotional, but also weaker and subject to fits of weeping once a month." Women are born to be mothers. Men are stronger, both physically and psychologically and so are fit for work and to play role of dominant partners in the men-women relationships. It is because of such notions that the education of women is considered not of as much significance as the education of men. But is it the right conclusion? We will now try to focus our attention on this question.

There is much divergence in the opinions regarding the basic biological differences between sexes. One viewpoint is that sex differences are biologically determined while the other viewpoint emphasises that the only difference between the sexes is reproduction. Only men can impregnate women and only women can give birth and lactate. It is true that one is born either male or female (not talking into consideration a small percentage of those born with no explicit sex or as eunuch). But there are six determinants of gender: (1) Chromosomes, XX for females and XY for males, (2) Gonads, testes in males and ovaries in females, (3) Hormone level, more androgens in males and more oestrogens and progesterone in females, (4) Internal accessory organs, which are the uterus and the organ of menstruation in female and the prostrate gland and seminal vesicles involved in the secretion of seminal fluid in male, (5) External genital appearance. (6) Assigned sex and rearing, usually based solely on external genital appearance (Hampson and Hampson, 1961).[1]

There is research evidence that indicates that after birth the brain regulates secretion of sex hormones. Puberty seems to be initiated by an interaction between the sex hormone and certain cells of the brain. In normal child, both male (androgen) and female (oestrogen) sex hormones are almost undetectable in the urine until the child is eight to ten years of age. At this point the male hormones sharply increase in both sexes, while the female hormones increase only in females. In girls the production of sex hormone becomes cyclic at about the eleventh year and is accompanied by the beginning of menstruation, the appearance of secondary sexual characteristics, and a growth spurt. Thus in terms of hormones there are no appreciable differences between males and females up to puberty. After puberty both adrogenic and oestrogenic hormones are present in both sexes but in different proportions. Males have high level of androgens and low level of oestrongens, while females have high level of oestrogens and moderate level of androgens.

A very relevant question that may be raised here is: Do hormones determine our personality and behaviour completely or in their determination social factors are also involved? The biological determinists consider that hormones give us energy and direct that energy into natural channel such as sex and fighting. Thus our moods and behaviour are related to our own body state and socialisation factor is irrelevant. But this view is open to controversy. Research has shown that even our private emotions and their interpretation are shaped by reaction of those around us. While visceral sensations such as heart palpitation, flushing and tremor tell us that we are emotionally aroused, we have to learn whether that arousal means that we are excited, angry or happy. All body chemical hormones produce a physiological state that must be translated into personality and behaviour through a specific social control. Thus sex role probably enters into the very way we perceive and interpret our own bodily sensation even those due to hormone. This is not to say that hormone levels are irrelevant to personality and behaviour. It merely suggests that even with such purely biological differences as hormones, we need to keep a sharp eye for ways in which social factors help to translate these biological factors into every day behaviour. We may say that the differences in personality and behaviour of male and female are not only because of hormones but also the process of socialisation of girls and boys creates such differential behaviour, which is known as typically male or female behaviour. We may give a few more research findings to establish our above-mentioned belief.

The hormone androgen is found in greater quantity in males than in females. This is then considered as a factor governing more assertive behaviour among males. But Moss (1967) found that mothers tend to comfort crying female babies more than they do crying male's.[2] It may be that the male infant experiences visceral sensation, such as stomach contractions of hunger pains. He cries but mother's attention is not drawn. He then learns that crying is not enough. He has to assert himself physically to attract the mother's attention. When this situation persists for months or years the male child may then associate this visceral sensation with greater activity or aggression and he may show it in his emotion of anger. On the other hand the female infant when experiences the similar visceral sensation due to stomach contraction she may also cry but in her case the mother comforts her. Gradually the female may come to associate these visceral sensations with comforting which may lead her to the emotion of happiness. The mothers perhaps do not attend to the male infant's cries as quickly as that of female infants because they may feel that males ought to be tough and should not cry. The finding of Moss may be taken with a sense of skepticism in the case of Indian male child. In this country because of too high aspirations for a male child more attention is given to him by the mother. But this might be leading the male child becoming too much attached to the mother and an entirely dependent individual to the parental wishes.

It cannot be said that hormone levels are irrelevant to personality and behaviour. It merely suggests that even in dealing with such purely biological differences as hormones, we need to keep a sharp eye for ways in which social factors help to translate these biological factors into day to day behaviour.

The controversy surrounding aggression is not about whether males act more aggressively than females but about the causes for these sex differences, for regardless of how aggression is defined and measured, males of all ages show a consistent tendency to be more aggressive than their female peers.[3-6] The greater male aggression is expressed not only in a variety of behavioural modes but also in a variety of situation and culture. But how do female hormones affect aggression? Unfortunately we know little about the answer to this question. Most researchers have assumed that male hormones increase aggression while female ones decrease it. Bronson and Desjardins[7] found that administering female hormones to newborn may decrease the aggressiveness of males but increase the aggressiveness of females. Thus in females the oestrogens may mimic the effect of androgens in males: when given to males, however, oestrogens may interfere with the action of the androgens.

Further more, male androgens administered shortly before or after birth seem to increase aggressive behaviour in females but not in males, while female hormones administered at that time also seem to increase aggressive behaviour in female while decreasing it in males. Thus XX hormones, whether androgens or oestrogens seem to increase aggressive behaviours in females more than in males. This conclusion then suggests that it is the absolute level of all hormones, androgens and oestrogens together, that underlies aggression in women, rather than a level of androgens relative to that of oestrogens. The basic argument is that both the sexes are actually equally aggressive in their underlying motivation but carry out desires to hurt others in different ways. This argument takes two basic forms. The first maintains that the two sexes are reinforced for different forms of aggression: Girls are allowed to show hostility only in subtle ways, while boys are encouraged to show it more directly by physical attack. The second form of argument maintains that aggression in general, is less acceptable and hence more discouraged for girls, leading to greater female anxiety and conflict over aggression.

It is now widely known that there are no sex differences in over all scores on intelligence tests. Some psychologists have, however, suggested that the sex hormones influence general intellectual capacity. The most popular view has been that male hormones enhance intellectual functioning and development in both sexes and perhaps is based on the assumption that, several social and physical behaviour levels of male hormones are related to aggressive or energetic intellect.[8] There are also some psychologists who argue that female hormones may underlie intellectual ability.[9]

The fact that males and females obtain similar overall scores on intelligence tests which does not mean that there are no sex differences in intellectual abilities. The pattern of intellectual abilities that make up the overall IQ score differs for the two sexes. In fact IQ tests are carefully constructed to weight the various portions on which men and women typically score higher in such a way that their average overall scores will be equivalent. Females generally excel in verbal ability while males in visual-spatial and mathematical ability. The females superiority in verbal is found in both "lower level" measure (fluency) and "higher level" tasks (comprehension of different material and creative writing). The male's visual-spatial advantage is about equal in non-analytical tasks (matching similar shapes and completing routine numerical operation, perceiving and manipulating parts and performing complex numerical operations).

The idea of difference in male and female brains continue to have popular appeal and has been hotly debated and researched for many decades in spite of numerous contradictions in both theory and data. About the differences between the male and female brains the researchers are only able to find that the issue is extremely complicated and does not offer any conclusive evidence that biological sex differences exist in intellectual performance.

Training the Intellect

Can the sex difference in intellectual abilities be erased through altered social experience or specific training? If they can, these differences might be attributed to differences in the training that males and females receive in the usual course of growing up in our culture.

Our entire educational system is based on the premise that training is crucial, that without it children would not be able to reason clearly or to complete complex verbal and non-verbal tasks. Yet every teacher knows that there is limit to what the best instruction can accomplish with each child. There seem to be a basic intellectual capacity that sets the limit for the rate and perhaps for the total amount of learning. With no instruction only a few children will develop complex skills, yet with the best instruction no all children will become highly skilled. The issue is whether instruction helps a child use basic cognitive abilities he/she already possesses, or whether instruction can affect the development of these basic intellectual abilities themselves.

Research on the training effect has focussed on the Embedded Figures Test (EFT) and the Rod Frame Test (RFT) developed by Witkin, in 1950. These tests assess spatial decontextualisation, or the ability to extract key elements of a stimulus from a confusing background. They measure "fields dependence versus fields independence" that is one's ability to assess external or internal stimulation independently of the environment. It has been reported that women are more fields dependent than men are. In other words, women have lower spatial ability scores than men have. It was also reported that the field independence does not increase with training. But these findings and interpretations have been challenged. Mary Brown Parlee (1973-74) conducted a thorough review of all published studies and concluded that sex differences were not nearly so conclusive as usually reported.[10] Parlee maintained that field independence scores tend to improve with practice or training.[11]

Cross-cultural research results lead to the conclusion that the greater field dependence in women is an indication both of basic female dependence on others for emotional support and social stimulation and of a general lack of "psychological differentiation" or development of a clearly defined and separate self-identity. Kogan and Kogan (1970) conclude that not only child rearing practices are associated with spatial ability scores in the predicted fashion, but sex roles are also implicated, i.e. men tend to score higher in spatial ability in those cultures with marked differences between the social roles assigned to the two sexes.[12] The assumption is that greater sex role differentiation is associated with greater encouragement of dependence in females, and this dependence in turn interferes with spatial ability as measured by field independence and other measures.

The cross-cultural argument is organised around the theme of dependence and assumes that the trait of dependence interferes with the restructuring of external physical and social stimulation and hence inhibits abstract reasoning. When cultures begin to adopt a modern lifestyle, allow children more autonomy, or define the proper role of the sexes less strictly, they are increasing the independence of their population. This more independent population then scores higher on field independence and other spatial ability measures. But increased childhood autonomy, decreased sex-role differentiation, and increased technological innovation are all associated with higher levels of formal education for the population in general and for women in particular. Thus increase in visual-spatial ability scores may be reflecting increased formal education rather than a personality trait of independence.

To conclude the argument regarding physiological differences influencing the intellectual differences between males and females we once again raise the question: Do biological sex differences underlie any possible differences? It seems unlikely. Owing to traditional sex roles females are discouraged from being assertive and independent and therefore, their intellectual development and performance are inhibited. It is very well known that the parents treat male and female newborns differently. They encourage gross motor behaviour in males while viewing females as littler, cuter, cuddlier, and generally more fragile. The cross-cultural research echoes this social theme by demonstrating that most cultures encourage males to be independent and assertive while encouraging females to be dependent, nurturing and responsible.

Education of Women in View of their Physiological Make-up

In 1912 in his book, *The Psychology of Education* Walton[13] wrote that the profound physiological differences which distinguish the sexes are the correlates of equally important mental differences. While man lives by reason, women's outlook is molded and determined by feeling. In his opinion the advocates and promoters of equal education to the sexes sadly ignore the mental and intellectual differences between the two sexes. He is against co-education. He emphasised that, as the psychological differences between man and woman are so intimate, so deep that the other cannot give the real training in character and in outlook in life of the one sex. A man cannot be a really sympathetic guide to a girl, nor a woman to a boy, simply because the man has never been neither a girl nor woman a boy. But Walton clarifies that it must never be supposed that woman is an imperfectly developed man. That woman differs from man in intellect does not mean that she is in any way intellectually inferior to him.

He proposes a different type of education for woman as her functions differ from that of man. He proposes a system of education which lays stress on preparation for an efficient wife's duties.

Howard in 1928 drew attention to the prevailing educational system in which the boys and girls studied very much the same things even when their schools were separate. He advocated a separate system of education for boys and girls. In his opinion girls are liable to fatigue more readily after puberty when the amount of haemoglobin in the blood becomes lessened. With their thinner blood with lowered content after puberty, they are nearer to the threshold of anaemia. These girls in general are not so strong physically as boys are. They are also highly-strung and liable to nervous strain, which possibly is associated with the fact that physiologically they are liable to heavier drains upon the circulating calcium of the blood. These considerations of the physiology of the girl, Howard advocates, must weigh when laying down a particular system of education for girls.[14]

Many other psychologists have also pointed out the physiological differences between men and women and recommended a different type of education for women. Geddes and Thompson in their book *Sex* (1927) argue that though certain differences between men and women are undoubtedly modification and natural, that is to say, the individual results of disparities or peculiarities in their education, training and occupations, many of the differences are constitutional, inborn and not acquired. They say that "the tenacity of life, the longer life, the characteristic endurance, the greater resistance to disease, the smaller percentage to genius, insanity, idiocy, suicide, and so on, are all correlated with the distinctively female constitution which may be theoretically regarded as relatively more constructive in its protoplasmic metabolism".[15]

Stanley Hall (1920) has stressed the psychological differentiation between man and woman. Woman, he points out, are more emotional, altruistic, intuitive, less judicial, and are less able to make disinterested and impersonal judgment. He is of the opinion that woman thinks more in terms of the concrete, is slower in logical thought and has less patience involved in science and invention.[16]

The psychologists, physiologists and social reformers till quite recently were pointing out the different physiological make-up of women as a ground for giving them a different type of education than that was to be given to men. They were emphasising that the existing female education was incompatible with the nature and need of woman. It had entirely ignored her function and mission in life, namely motherhood. The educational curriculum for her was a complete imitation of that of the man, as if like him she was going to be in future an office bearer. With only a few exceptions most of the women were going to be married and the motherhood was an undoubted fact. Hence they needed an education which would prepare them for motherhood. These persons were quite critical of the modern feminists whom they considered were criminally ignoring this vital fact in their zest of following the standards of male pursuits. According to them the girls should be given education in domestic economy, nursing of children, hygiene of pregnancy, general household management, and in all such subjects which would be intimately personal to them.

Dr. Saleeby in *the Report of the Proceedings of the English Speaking Conference on Infant Mortality* has remarked: "Education of a girl must be to prepare her for womanhood and not to show that at a pinch she would be a boy".[17]

Truby King in the same report has mentioned that: "proper education should be given but above all there must be a development of love of human life, and interest in children, and a development of proper womanly qualities".[18]

The ideas expressed above are considered redundant now. The technological and scientific advancement has refuted all the arguments put as above in view of the women's physiology. It is now being said that because of technology, tomorrow's most challenging and rewarding careers will require the powers of mind, not muscles. The most modern psychological and brain research have made it very clear, despite all of yesterday's cliches, that women have all the intellect and ambition needed to go after these jobs. Science is also relieving the women from the tyranny of the biological clock, allowing women the freedom to delay bearing children until late thirties or sixties.

The changes in work and reproductive choices are revamping women's family lives, encouraging "Parallel" marriages in which husband and wife both share the work within and outside the home.

The study of biological and other sex differences is being carried out on many fronts by the anthropologists and psychologists, who catalog human behaviour, neuroscientists, who probe the brain, and endocrinologists, who trace the action of hormones in the body. It is still a very young science. But this science has given us new dimension regarding the biological and psychological differences between man and woman.

Male and female brains are different although not in ways that would support most of the stereotypes of the past. The distinction is certainly not one of intelligence, for the average female brain is as smart as the average male brain by whatever test we use to measure it. The difference lies in question of values, interests, style and motivation. Different does not mean superior or inferior. We should also not deny biology in order to shake off the myths that have accumulated regarding female nature. Howard Gardner in his book *Frames of Mind* (1983) argues that the human intellect is not a single entity. Multiple forms of intelligence exist, including musical, linguistic, spatial, logical-----mathematical, interpersonal and bodily and kinesthetic intelligences. All individuals have an intellectual mix that includes all these types in varying proportions. The mix may be weighted differently in each sex too.[19]

The genetic engineering has revealed a number of facts regarding the physiological development of male and female. Now the scientists recognise that the creation of a male from the arrival of the chromosome to the testosterone that floods the embryo, is a precarious business, the result, at best, is a creature with a single survival advantage over females; greater muscular strength. At every stage of life, men pay dearly to gain this advantage; fall victim to every threat from genetic defects to heart disease. Women are biologically superior to men in every other category but muscles. Boys are more likely to suffer than girls from birth defects and genetic diseases. So called *X*-linked genetic diseases such as haemophilia and muscular dystrophy strike boys almost exclusively because they are carried on the *X*-chromosome to protect them. But *Y* provides no such back up to a boy with a defective *X* Infant boys suffer more illness and infection, and in the first month of life three of them die for every two-baby girl. At every age, women have lower death rates from heart disease and heart attacks than do men. Even women who have high blood pressure and high blood cholesterol do not die as readily as men do. Women are less likely to die of infectious diseases. The endocrinologist Estelle Ramey says: "So women are an extraordinarily viable sex, right from the moment of conception".[20]

In the modern times medicine has reduced the perils of childbirth and the threat of infectious diseases. Women are simply better prepared mentally and physically, to meet the pace and challenges of life and work in a technologically advanced world.

Women of all ages have more responsive immune systems than men, giving them protection from bacteria and virus. Girls have higher levels of a protective blood protein called immunoglobulin M or IgM than males, and a gene on the X-chromosome seems to be responsible for the immune system. The X-chromosome also carries other genes that influence various parts of the defense system. And after puberty, oestrogens increase the efficiency of the immune responses.

It is becoming increasingly clear as the gap between men's and women's life expectancies grown ever wider that women have better ways of coping with stress, physically, mentally and socially. Some of the biggest risks to life today—heart disease, alcoholism, lung cancer, suicide—arise from the way we handle pressure and stress. Although the same stress response takes place in both men and women it is more extreme in men because they need a bigger head of steam to get their larger muscles fueled for action. It has been found that women are about fifteen years behind men in accumulating significant heart damage. Men, on average, start to develop heart disease between the age of thirty-five and forty, women between the ages of fifty and fifty-five. Men between thirty-five and fifty-five are twice as likely to die of heart disease as are women. Today's women are entering into competitive athletics with the same intensity as men and their performance is improving dramatically. No doubt that there are some biological differences between the sexes that cannot be ignored, although they are not nearly as great as the myths about the women have been propagating.

Knowledge is the most precious commodity in the information age. The doors are now wide open for women to push against the frontiers of ignorance and it is very heartening to note that women have begun to take their mental and intellectual capabilities seriously. Keeton and Basrin in their book *Women of Tomorrow* (1985) write that women are forging new ways to care, applying their concern along with their intellect to much larger human goals. These authors emphasise that women can be system analysts and computer programmers, they can be hardware as well as software engineers; women can enter into the fields of infertility and test-tube baby research, of molecular biology and genetic engineering; women should prefer to study Bionics, (a field that's already produced artificial hearts, artificial pancreases to secrete insulin to diabetics, the first rudimentary artificial ears and eyes connected directly to the human brain, etc.). It's never too late for a woman to start to find a place for herself in any of these frontier fields. The country needs scientists and engineers to improve life on earth and help expand in space.[21]

It can be said with confidence on the basis of the findings of various physiologists and the biologists that the women are not physiologically weak, rather they are by nature superior and their superiority lies in their power to give birth. It is argued that woman and woman alone have the capacity to give birth. Despite all the evolution of socio-economic conditions and progress of genetic manipulation of medical knowledge, the fact remains that it is the woman and none else that carries the work of reproduction. It is this biological feature gifted by nature to woman, which is at the root of the existence of necessary minimal sexual division of labour.

The modern physiologists reject biological explanation of the inferior status of woman. They argue that the biological view does explain why men have been excluded from the task of reproduction, but it fails to clarify why women have been excluded from some activities, which are not reproductive. This implies that the inferior position of the women is not due to any natural deficiency in them but it has resulted from changing historical circumstances, which have always been tied to the reproductive role. Needless to say in the modern society, women have been doing the same work that was once considered exclusively to be of men's. For instance, women have gone to space, joined modern guerrilla groups and fought on the battle fronts, headed the country's administration, participated in sports and games and the like. To the chagrin of men, women even surpass men in many of the so-called men's activities. Hence it does not stand to reason to attribute women's inferiority in society to biological or physical factors.

In view of the above mentioned facts we may suggest that the education for women must be as liberal and deep as for men. A women must know the course of history, the rise and fall of different political systems, the co-ordination and contact of different cultures, the fundamental issues that this evolution in history involves. She must also know where she stands, how is she related to society, how can she promote solidarity in social life without injuring the growth of the individual. She must also know how life began. She must have knowledge of Botany and Zoology. She must learn Geography and Literature, which are the fountains of culture and civilisation. In short she must learn all the areas of liberal education so that she knows her relations to the society and may thus prepare herself for real citizenship.

The woman must also have training in domestic hygiene and economy. She must learn the art of nursing children and decoration of home. She may also learn fine arts, dancing and music. Her education thus must equip her for the twin task of keeping the household and involving herself in the world of work. We consider that system of education as an ideal one which aims at making of each individual a versatile artisan—versatile for changing conditions, a good citizen consciously playing a part in a general scheme and a well-disposed, considerate person in full possessions of all his/her powers.

The education of the women should usher in an era of complete rationalism and equality. Equality between men and women means equality in their dignity and worth as human beings as well as equality in their rights, opportunities and responsibilities.[22]

REFERENCES

1. J.L. Hampson and J.G. Hampson, "The ontogenesis of sexual behaviour in man." In *Sex and Internal Secretions* (Vol. ii) ed. by W.C. Young, (Baltimore, 1961), pp. 1401-32.
2. H.A. Moss, "Sex, age, and state as determinants of mother-infant interaction." *Merrill-Palmer Quarterly 13: 29-36 edited reproduction in Readings in the Psychology of Woman*, ed. by J.M. Bardwick, (New York, 1972), pp. 22-29.
3. E.E. Maccoby and C.N. Jacklin, *The Psychology of Sex Differences*, (Stanford, Cal., 1974).
4. W. Mischel, Sex typing and socialization. In Carmichael's *Manual of Child Psychology* (3rd edition, Vol. 2) ed. by P.H. Mussen, (New York, 1970), pp. 3-72.
5. R.M. Oetzel, "Classified summary research in sex differences." In *The Development of Sex Differences*, ed. by E.E. Maccoby, (Stanford, Cal., 1966), pp. 323-51.

6. L.M. Terman and L.E. Tyler, "Psychological sex differences." In *Manual of Child Psychology*, ed. (2nd edition) by L. Carmichael, (New York, 1954).
7. F.H. Bronson and C. Desjardins, "Aggression in adult mice: Modification of neonatal injections of gonadal hormones." *Science* 161 (1968), pp. 705-6.
8. A.A. Ehrhardt and J. Money, "Progestin-inducted hermaphroditism: IQ and psychosexual identity in study of ten girls." *Journal of Sex Research 3 (1)* (1967), 83-100.
9. K. Dalton, "Ante-natal progesterone and intelligence." *British Journal of Psychiatry 114* (1968), pp. 1377-82.
10. M.B. Parlee, "Sex differences in perceptual field dependence: A look at some data embedded in theory." *Unpublished Manuscript, Radcliffe Institute (1973-74).*
11. M.B. Parlee.
12. J. Kogan and N. Kogan, "Individual variation in cognitive processes." In *Carmichael's Manual of Psychology. 3rd edition*, pp. 1273-1305.
13. J.Welton, *The Psychology of Education.*, (1912) pp. 128-135. Quoted in Y.M. Rege. *Whither Woman*, (Bombay, 1938), p. 210.
14. Howard, *The Mixed School*, (1928). Quoted in Y.M. Rege, pp. 213-15.
15. Geddes and Thompson, *Sex* (1927). Quoted in Y.M. Rege, pp. 216-217.
16. Stanely Hall, *Educational Problems*. Vol. 1. Quoted in Y.M. Rege, p. 249.
17. Saleeby, *Report of the Proceeding of the English-speaking conference on Infant Mortality*. p. 295. Quoted in Y.M. Rege, p. 239.
18. Truby King, Quoted in Y.M. Rege, p. 239.
19. Howard Gardner. *Frames of Mind (1983).*
20. Estelle Ramey, Quoted in Kathy Keeton and Yvonne Basrin, *Women of Tomorrow*, (New York, 1985), p. 63.
21. Kathy Keeton and Yvonne Basrin, *Women of Tomorrow*, pp. 231-45.
22. Usha Batra. "Psycho-social and Philosophical Dimensions of Women Education in India and the Projection of Futuristic Trends: A theoretical Study." Un*published Ph.D. thesis* submitted to Panjab University, (Chandigarh, 1997), p. 1: 31.

8

SOCIO-PSYCHOLOGICAL DETERMINANTS OF WOMEN EDUCATION

The Indian world is a male world with ambivalent attitude towards female. She is visualised as good and noble as well as bad and degenerative. Her reproductive functions are worshipped, but her sex is considered as a pull towards hell. She is respected as mother but hated as charmer. Still the Indian male wishes to enjoy her sex in every conceivable manner as is depicted in temple designs, architecture, erotic texts and in the pornographic material. Literature depicts his enjoyment; his keenness to impregnate her and to father many children even though they may be deprived of food and milk and live in abject poverty. The female submits herself to the male's demands because she believes she must serve him and raise the offspring she is destined to bear. She is absolutely dependent on male for her well-being. The willingness of the female for male domination, for letting him enjoy her body without her desire for it, for bearing children without having strength to endure pregnancy or money to feed them is explained by the fact that her life is woven into the myth of motherhood and service to man whom she has been conditioned to be economically dependent. Her weakness makes it obligatory for her to seek male protection and male in turn considers it as his birthright to hold the positions of power and authority over her.

The most vital questions which the modern psychologists and sociologists are concerned with are: Why are Indian women, even the educated ones, not prepared to emerge free from their mythical existence? Why are they submitting to the irrational male domination? Why are the Indian women still not prepared to lead a free and independent life? To seek answers to these questions we will have to peep into the psyche of the Indian women. To do so we will have to revert back to the women in ancient India?

There is no doubt in it that the ancient Aryan women were strong willed and domineering. The traces of domination can be found in the lives of the famous and respected women of ancient India. Hence it may be possible that the psyche of the Indian women is an offshoot of an urge to dominate. This may sound to be a view very much different from the prevailing opinion. But it has many elements of truth. We will present some arguments and facts in favour of this viewpoint.

The powerful and strong women of ancient India, when controlled by scheming males contrived a way to seek satisfaction. Pardweshi, the wife of blind Rishi Drighatamas, threw him in the river when he proposed legislation that a woman should have only one husband in her life. She was not prepared to subordinate her sexuality to the whims of one male. Drighatamas saved himself by clinging to a raft and lived long enough to put through his proposals. Later women were bound by this law and were unable to physically revolt because of weakness due to frequent pregnancies and domestication. These women learned to achieve supremacy not by trying to break the myths, but by strengthening them. They did not make demands, but submitted to the demands of men. As the men continued to assert themselves, the strands of the web increased and women internalised their domination and externalised their subordination until their external life became miserable and their interal life gained expression through entirely different channels.

Indian woman serves her husband and rears her

children and finds happiness in being half-clad and half-fed so that her husband and children get the best. Then her son marries and she demands a great price for rearing him up in the form of dowry. When the daughter-in-law enters the house, the mother-in-law's dominant attitude becomes explicit. Many stories depict the harshness with which the mother-in-law treats her son's wife. In some marriage customs, the mother of the son runs out of the house and sits on the edge of a well ready to jump in until the son and daughter-in-law offer their devotion and shower her with gifts. Thus the urge for domination which she has repressed when she entered the house as a young bride now finds as outlet, as she becomes the domineering mother-in-law.

The strict supervision and harsh moral codes under which women rear their daughters may also be outlets of the dominant urge. The Indian woman judges other women's behaviour patterns under strict social norms. Any failing on the part of another woman is a delight because it establishes her own moral superiority. By scandalising other she obtains a sense of power. No wonder that women gossip has become such powerful instrument for the maintenance of the status quo. Any change in existing norm releases dormant energy for domination.

We have made an earlier reference to the predominance of an element of masochism in the Indian female. This elements is her weapon for dominance. She stoops to conquer and often becomes successful. Consequently, her husband becomes more sadistic and tries to crush her further. She submits to her cruelty and thus shows superiority in endurance. Thus, a vicious cycle ensues.

Women's desire for dominance is a secret hidden desire. It is not evident at the external level of her existence but an analysis of her behaviour pattern throughout her life reveals it. Woman learns from early life that she is liked if she is helpless and dependent. She gets her needs met from her father and brothers when she subordinates herself completely and serves them devotedly. She learns that her path to any type of fulfillment lies through them. She also notices that her prestige and way of life depend on her docility. She, therefore, represses her will for independent thinking. She becomes completely domesticated and all her desire for dominance find an outlet in leading a subordinated home life.

Carstairs while carrying on her study of "village women of Rajasthan" was warned by the men of the village that their submissive women were really quite strong-minded and often get their own way. The women even employed witchcraft. Carstairs says: "At first, I found it almost inconceivable that these meek, seemingly unassertive women could be seen as powerful agents of the supernatural; but on 7th March, 1950, I witnessed a scene which revealed them in a rather different light".[1] That night when all the men of the village, except Carstairs and an invalid old man, left the village for joining a wedding party the women came out of their houses and with gay abandon indulged in dancing, singing, abusing and rehearsing many of the sexual acts. They were unbridled, strong in their expressions; and as fully emancipated as women in any part of the world can be. The next day Carstairs found their behaviour dull and demure. Carstairs writes: "Next day the wedding party returned from Togi, and the women of Sujarupa resumed their normal demure behaviour; but I felt that I had been shown a glimpse of quite a different side of their nature, one rarely given free expression".[2]

It must be that Indian women have developed the art of concealing the extrovert side of their nature. From their external behaviour it is difficult to fathom their psyche. One must patiently go deeper into the analysis of their behaviour pattern. It is firmly asserted that they are neither treacherous nor evil. There has, however, developed some complexity in their behaviour promoted by the sadistic attitudes of the men and suppressed feelings of the women for the ages.

In all the normal human beings, both the attitudes of dominance and submission may be found. Both are necessary for survival. In women, submission is overt, while in the men, dominance is external. But covertly, neither the domination in women nor the submission in men is completely lost. Women learn to submit in order to dominate, and men learn to dominate in order to submit. Thus it may be wrong to contend that the Indian world is absolutely a male world. It is true that men have the economic power but this is what the women desire. Until they learn to desire overtly their own freedom and independence the situation regarding their status and position is not going to change. Here is then a challenge for those who plan for women education in our country. They have to plan for a different cultural training than that which is prevalent today.

We may again repeat that domination and submission are a universal part of nature. When one is confronted by physical danger, the instinct of self-preservation leads him to choose either to fight or flee. Some animals play "possum" and pretend they are dead until their predator leaves. Others attack ferociously. Pardweshi made an attempt to fight. Women after her learned to be more careful and played possum. They took flight in the inner dorms of their psyche and wage a battle in which their unconscious played the part of warrior who fought not with weapons of destruction, but with the weapons of seduction and devotion. If the Indian women are satisfied with the situation as described above then why bother to change it? If she is dominant in her own way, why consider her the weaker sex? To find satisfactory answers to these questions the following consequences of her above described behaviour pattern must be taken into consideration. The most important consequence is that the development of the psyche of the Indian woman takes place in the direction of creating a split personality. The person who is responsible to subdue her becomes her passion. She becomes too ritualistic, superstitious and superficial. She becomes too modest and looses all her initiative in taking decisions. Her life becomes one of rigidity and ignorance. She curbs independent thinking not only in herself but also in her daughter and other female relatives. She develops intolerance to any deviant member of her own sex. She becomes ruthless with her dependent relatives, particularly towards those women who are either divorced or widows.

Indian men respect motherhood in their women folk while women seem to want to turn their husbands into little boys so that they can "mother" them. The women want their men to be completely dependent on them to fulfill their needs. This type of behaviour pattern may be at the root of Indians lapses in taking bold decisions in the hours of crises and in the development of the "killer instinct" in the competitive games and competitive enterprises. They very often lose control even in the win-win situations.

The subordination of the Indian women served the purpose of securing for them the protection they needed so that they might avoid hardships for themselves and their children. Aileen Ross writes:

> "The attitude of Hindu women to this subordinate position has not often been understood by Western observers, for they have seldom seen it in the context of the total family setting. Bachmann interprets the satisfaction, which the Hindu women did, in fact, derive from her seemingly 'low' position. He describes Kasturbai, Gandhi's wife: 'Whoever knows her is bound to believe that the self-surrender of the widow which led to the custom of self-immolation on the funeral pyre, must in certain cases have been quite voluntary".[3]

The Indian women are considered downtrodden, but to a great extent they are exercising their own will to this effect. They must now understand through proper education and training that the subordination might have been prudent in the past and the tension relieving in the present, but it is no longer necessary for the Indian women to submit to it. They must reflect upon on to what they desire and develop enough strength to achieve their goals of life. They must purge out old orthodox traditions and adapt to the modern world. It is satisfying to note that quite a few modern educated women are taking initiative in achieving their economic independence and in the free exercise of their will power. They are showing their excellence in very diverse fields. There are at present almost all the avenues of work or activities in which they are competing with men and achieving success. No doubt there are still a large number of women who are living the life of drudgery and toil mostly because of lack of initiative on their part and due to their ignorance. Hence the educational system in this country is facing the gigantic task of emancipation and empowerment of such women.

Eleanor Maccoby and Carol Jacklin (1974) reviewed and integrated the extensive research literature on psychological sex differences, reading through some 2,000 books and articles in the process. Most of these studies were comparisons of male and female behaviour in infancy and childhood, rather than in adulthood. On the basis of their review, they concluded that many of the differences that are commonly believed to exist between males and females are in fact myths. For example, there is no good evidence that boys are more independent, ambitious or achievement oriented than girls or that girls are more nurturant, sociable or suggestible than boys are. On the whole Maccoby and Jacklin conclude that male and female are much more similar to one another than they are different, and they share the same fundamental needs, emotions and abilities.[4]

If many of the stereotypical differences between the sexes are myths, then why are they perpetuated? The main reason for the perpetuation of the myths seems to be the different opportunities that society provides for men and women. In fact, as children grow up, boys undoubtedly become more politically and professionally ambitious than girls, and girls become more interested in taking care of children. The differences that we observe probably result from social values and opportunities, rather than from basic psychological differences.

Our expectations about what men and women should do and what they should like are called sex roles. Boys are encouraged to be ambitious and assertive and discouraged from expressing their weaknesses or their tender feelings. Girls on the other hand learn to play a more submissive and dependent role. They are taught to be well-behaved and co-operative and to act as if they have no aggressive impulses at all. Girls are also expected to be tender and nurturing. These expectations are effectively communicated to the sons and daughters. This communication is sometimes done directly by suggesting the desired behaviour to the child and by rewarding the child for performing it. In addition, once the child learns his or her sex which all children do by age three, the child invariably wants to demonstrate that he or she can behave like a member in good standing of that sex.

Changing Sex Roles

As we are marching towards 21st century, the growing age of computer technology, the psychologists and sociologists are coming to the conclusion that traditional sex roles are in need of change. They have come to believe that by putting people in slots labelled 'male' and 'female' and shaping them to fit the slots we are limiting their full development as human beings. Instead they propose that each child should be treated as a total person, without regard for the traditional notions of what a boy or girl should be.

It may, however, be also noted that as the idea of breaking down traditional roles has gained force, there has also been a great deal of opposition to it. It is argued that sex roles are based on biological differences that have evolved over the course of millions of years and, therefore, should not be tempered with. In his book *Sexual Suicide*, George Gilder (1973) writes:

> "When reforming the roles of men and women, we must always be careful to avoid gibberish-patterns of activity that so violates the inner constitution of the species that they cannot be integrated with our irreducible human natures" [5]

Gilder's warning may have some validity, but recent research findings reduce the force of his arguments. Maccoby and Jacklin emphasise that psychological differences between men and women are small, and they are based on only a slight degree of biological predispositions. Considerable change in sex roles could be accomplished by changing our values and expectations, without negation of our biological nature.[6]

A second argument against sex-role changes is the notion that if boys and girls do not develop the pattern of traits that are appropriate for their sex, they may become confused about their sexual identity and thereby run the risk of serious maladjustment.

But recent research provides little cause for such alarm. Virtually all girls and boys learn without much trouble which sex they belong to and they do this by the time they are three years old. The extensive sex-role training that follows is not necessary to develop a stable sexual identity. In addition, highly 'masculine' males and highly 'feminine' females are not better adjusted or healthier than people who are less highly sex-typed.[7]

Sandra Bem (1975) has called the ability to behave in ways traditionally associated with both sexes—Psychological androgyny. An androgynous person is one who combines 'masculine' and 'feminine' behaviours. Bem has measured androgyny by asking students how often various adjectives are descriptive of themselves. Some of the adjectives were traditionally masculine, as for example, ambitious, self-reliant, and independent. Some were traditionally feminine like affectionate, gentle, sensitive. Subjects were categorised as androgynous if they indicated that they are about equally well-described by masculine and feminine traits. Bem found that androgynous students of both sexes behaved more effectively in a variety of laboratory situations than students who were highly masculine or highly feminine. The androgynous men and women could be independent and assertive when they needed to be men or women. They were also responsive in appropriate situations. They were able to behave in a more flexible and humane manner.[8]

The above finding has very significant implications for schooling. Some schools keeping in mind the value of androgynous personality have started to provide work experiences for boys and girls in order to develop the dignity of labour in them and to accommodate reciprocal roles. Some co-educational institutions have introduced cooking, homecraft and embroidery for both boys and girls in their curriculum. They are providing the same type of curriculum for both boys and girls. It is desirable that almost all the schools should provide such a curriculum, which do not discriminate between the two sexes.

In spite of various measures, which have been taken for ameliorating the conditions of the Indian women there is still much scope for reforms? Unless such customs, traditions, rituals and values and attitudes which view and treat women as inferior beings and less desirable than men are discarded and changed, the status and position of the Indian women are not going to improve. This change can be brought about through equalitarian, formal and informal education. Education must prepare both the sexes for becoming all that they can be without any discrimination or prejudice.

REFERENCES

1. G. Morris Carstairs, "Village Women of Rajasthan," in *Indian Women*, ed. By Devaki Jain, (New Delhi, 1975), p. 233.
2. Carstairs, p. 235.
3. Aileen D. Ross, *The Hindu Family in its Urban Setting*, (Toronto, 1961), p. 105.
4. E.E. Maccoby and C.N. Jacklin, *The Psychology of Sex Differences*, (Stanford, Cal., 1974).
5. George Gilder, "Sexual Suicide," (Quadrangle, 1973) in Elton B. Mcneil and Zick Rubin, *The Psychology of being Human*, (San Francisco, 1977), p. 109.
6. George Gilder.
7. Usha Batra, Psycho-social and Philosophical Dimensions of Women Education in India and the Projection of Futuristic Trends: A Theoretical Study, *Unpublished Ph.D. thesis* submitted to Panjab University, (Chandigarh, 1997), pp. 161-162.
8. Sandra Bem (1975) quoted in *Ph.D. Thesis* by Usha Batra.

9

SOCIO-PSYCHOLOGICAL DETERMINANTS OF THE EDUCATION OF DALIT WOMEN

In the previous chapter we have described the socio-psychological factors which are influencing the education of the Indian women. In considering Indian women we have kept in our frame of reference a Hindu middle class woman. But Indian society is a very stratified one. There are many castes, classes and religions. The women belonging to upper and lower castes, rich and poor classes and Hindus, Muslims and Christians have there own specific problems even though as women they suffer from all those limitations with which the average woman of Hindu middle class suffers. In the present and the next chapters we are paying special attention to the problems concerning education of Dalit women and the women of the minority communities specially the Muslim women.

We are using the term Dalit women for all those women who are either put in the category of Harijans or Schedule Castes. These women suffer from many types of social disadvantages. Some of them were considered untouchable while in the case of most of them the food touched by them was considered as defiled by the caste Hindus. Many of these indignities have now been sought to be abolished by the legal measures, but still their lot is far from satisfaction. One of the important reasons for this state of affairs is the woeful neglect of their education. Their ignorance is the major threat to their existence. Why has their education suffered? What were the factors are still existing which have pushed them into a miserable existence? What factors which are putting hindrances in their respectable right of living? The thesis of this book is that these factors have to be searched out in the socio-psychological make-up of the women, particularly in relation to their education.

The Dalits have been put at the lowest level in the caste hierarchy of the Hindus. They were required to serve the higher castes. We are not entering into any discussion here as how and why this happened. This has already been a subject of a large number of investigations and discussions. Our concern here is that how this has affected the psyche of Dalits as well as the upper castes.

The Dalits were constantly reminded that they were the objects of hatred and their salvation lied in the service of the upper castes. This was done sometimes by persuasion but most of the times by force by the Brahamanical order of the Hindu society. They were told that they must have committed some heinous crimes or evil actions in their past life and hence they are born as "untouchables". This developed in them a feeling of inferiority complex and they began to consider themselves as the inferior specimen of the mankind. This feeling was much more aggravated among the females of the Dalits since they were considered inferior to their own men. The Dalit women accepted their lower status and position and started believing that it was fated that they involve themselves in doing menial tasks. Since these tasks required no education or training they developed a mentality that education is meant for the upper and richer castes and not for them. They thus never made an attempt to send their children to the schools. Also the higher castes did not allow Dalit children to sit with their own children in the schools and there were no schools exclusively set up for Dalit children.

The literacy rate in India according to the census of 1991 was 52.11 per cent. The percentage of male literacy was 63.86 while that of female was 39.42 only. According to the census report of 1981 the general female literacy percentage was 24.82. The literacy percentage of scheduled caste females was as low as 10.93 and of scheduled tribe females was 8.04 (Census was not conducted in Assam and no castes were scheduled by the President of India for Nagaland, A and N Islands and Laskhadweep and no tribes were scheduled in Haryana, Jammu and Kashmir, Punjab, Chandigarh, Delhi and Pondicherry). These figures show that the education of the Dalit women was totally neglected.

The Dalit women were mostly working in the unorganised sector. In the organised sector their percentage was quite low. There were only two scheduled caste women in Indian Foreign Services in 1987 while the number of male scheduled castes was 65. The male scheduled tribes numer was 30 while that of the females was 5 only. Similar was the case in most of the other Central services. In all the Central services while the total number of the women employed was 994 in the year 1987 only 31 were scheduled caste women and 31 scheduled tribe women.[1]

The employment prospects for Dalit women in the organised sector are very few. These women neither have the educational nor technical qualifications and nor have contacts or social connections. They have also to face discrimination from two directions. One is that they are women and the second that they belong to low strata of the society. Hence in spite of the reservations for schedule castes and backward classes the benefit do not reach up to them. Hence most of the Dalit women in the urban areas are self-employed in the areas like hawking, scrap collection, domestic help, petty trade, etc. The women have to undertake such employment for their survival and for supporting their families. The income from such jobs is very meagre and also has uncertainties. There is no security also in these types of activities. Some Dalit women are also employed in wage employment activities. These activities include construction labour, earthwork, petty manufacturing activities like beedi making or candle making etc. They are employed by some traders in these activities and are being paid very low wages. In the rural areas the Dalit women are engaged for labour in agriculture and agro-based industries.

From the brief account of the education and employment of the Dalit women it may be evident that in spite of more than 50 years of our independence they are in miserable plight. It is, therefore, necessary for the government as well as the general public that serious efforts are made towards their betterment. We can tackle this problem only when we make all out efforts for their education. One way to do it is to open more and more schools for them and give them incentives like free tuition, dress and mid-day meals. But this is a very simple solution. The women may still not go to attend the school. The majority of the Dalit households will not send their girls of school going age to the schools as this may mean the loss of income for the family as these girls might have been employed in some type of wage earning work or these girls might be busy in looking after their younger siblings, etc. when their parents have left for work. If we wish to educate them and provide help in their social and economic progress we must understand their psychology and the sociological problems which they face.

Psychological Aspects of the Education of Dalit Women

The Dalit women suffer from extensive inferiority complex. The indignities that they have suffered in the past have left such a deep mark on their psyhe that they had started considering themselves as persons meant to lead a miserable life. This complex has not been altered till the present times. Hardly they take interest in raising their pattern of life. The Dalit leaders have recently made very powerful efforts to bring changes in their thinking. Mayawati and Phoolan Devi are the present day examples of such leaders. But still there is a long way to go before the mentality of Dalit women as the scum of the society is going to change. The efforts of social workers and political leaders are undermined from time to time by the atrocities being committed on them by the upper caste and affluent members of the society. The tradition bound society in India do not relish that the Dalit women should think themselves as equal to them. They are prepared to commit all sorts of acts of aggression on them if they express any desire to achieve equality with the higher caste women.

The daily newspaper are full of incidents describing rapes, murders, and beatings of both the Dalit males and females. These have two types of reactions. One is that the Dalit leaders raise Dalit Sena and try to retaliate by attacking the citadels of the upper castes and the seconds that they take it as a matter of their fate. Both are the wrong approaches. The Sena approach increases caste tensions without offering any solution. The other approach of it being their fate is the pessimistic outlook that throws them back to square one. A better approach is to educate them in terms of their importance. They should not feel marginalised. It is the duty of their leaders to educate them in terms of their importance in the present day social and political order.

One of the factors responsible for their poor economic condition is the large number of children, which they produce. They do not realise that more children mean more mouths to feed. Unfortunately the Dalit leadership has failed to develop among Dalit women the value of family planning. The syndrome of what is fated will happen need to be altered. We may call such a syndrome as "fate-linked proverty syndrome". Unless the Dalit women are prepared to discard this syndrome their plight will remain the same.

Sociological Aspects

As we have already pointed out the Dalit women's low status and position is due to their poverty and involvement in menial tasks. To improve their lot it is necessary that they should get better education and training. Now no task may be taken as menial. The technology has created a situation in which even the most menial task can be performed with machines. The handling of machines is the task of the technologists. The technologists are those who have got training in the handling of the machines. Thus the women are to be trained in handling machines and in the use of gadgets. One example may be given to clarify the issue raised here. We all know that Barber or Nai caste was considered among the low castes. His job was hair cutting, etc. Today this role has been taken up by the so-called beauticians or by the owners of "air conditioned hair cutting saloons." The hair grooming is no more considered as a low task. Similar is the case with cooking. Now Chef is an honourable member of the society. The change has been brought about by the introduction of the specialised training being associated with these professions.

The Dalit women's aspirations and the motivations have to be increased manifolds. For this the social workers have to strive hard. The politicians cannot perform this task because they only want to keep their leadership intact or to get Dalit votes in the election. They have a vested interest in keeping the electorate ignorant and keeping it in the state in which it is so that these leaders can always exploit it by arousing its emotions for caste or class struggle. The enlightened electorate may question their leadership and may ask them to be accountable to the electorate. Only the leaders gain by creating hatred among different castes and classes. We may say that all the leaders are not like this. There are many selfless workers. It is to them that an appeal to bring a change in the psychology of the Dalits should be made.

The role of teachers in bringing attitudinal changes among the Dalit women cannot be ignored. Education does not mean simply learning the language or some other subjects. Real education is that which has a bearing on a better personal and social life of that individual who is getting education. It is, therefore, very important that those teachers are appointed in the schools where the Dalit children are studying who are dedicated to the task of freeing the Dalits from the syndrome of linked poverty.

REFERENCES

1. M.M. Rehman and Kamalkanta Biswal. *Education, Work and Women*, (New Delhi, 1993), pp. 108-09.
2. P.G. Jogdand (edited), Dalit Women, Issues and Perspectives, (New Delhi, 1995).
3. P.C. Jain, Shashi Jain and Sudha Bhatnagar (edited). *Scheduled Caste Women*, (Jaipur, 1997).

10

SOCIO-PSYCHOLOGICAL DETERMINANTS OF THE EDUCATION OF THE WOMEN OF THE MINORITY COMMUNITIES

In the Indian situation the education of the minority communities have been very much neglected except perhaps in the case of the Christian community. The worst sufferers are the women of the Muslim community. Because of poverty and *purdah* the Muslims have avoided sending their daughters to the schools. The Muslim clergy is by and large opposed to the liberal education of the girls. According to them the education of the women should be confined to the reading of the religious texts and to those activities which are performed by them for the maintenance of their households.

The Christians on the other hand, have a tradition of educating their daughters. The missionaries have opened a number of good institutions where the Christian girls get quality education. The girls of the Sikh minority except of the Sikhs who fall in the category of Dalits are able to get fairly good education. Hence the Muslim minority is the one which has not been able to educate its daughters to the extent to which they should have been educated. We shall examine in this chapter the socio-psychological factors that have affected the education of the Muslim girls.

The Muslims feel that it is ordained in holy book Quoran that the women are kept under *purdah*. It is often quoted:

And say to the believing women
That they should lower
Their gaze and guard
Their modesty; that they
Should not display their
Beauty and ornaments except
What (must ordinarily) appear thereof.
(Quoran 24:31)

According to the above verse among Muslim women veiling or *Purdah* is projected as the preferred code of conduct. They are supposed to remain veiled whenever they go out or face the males. They are thus restricted to go to those institutions in which they have to discard their veil. The choice of schooling, therefore, remains very limited. Because of *pardah* Muslim women are also restricted from undertaking jobs in the factories or offices. Their rightful place is considered home and their responsibilities are the domestic work and rearing of the children. It is, therefore, not surprising that very few Muslim women are employed in Government or factories or business services.

It may be mentioned that the Muslim community in India has undergone the trauma of partition. No doubt that to some extent the community in India was partly responsible for the partition of the country in 1947 but once it took place this community suffered a lot. Its elitist, well to do members, shifted to Pakistan and those who were left were separated from many of their near and dear once who migrated to Pakistan. The trauma of partition that separated the families is very effectively projected in the movie *Garam Hawa*. The affluent businessman of shoe market at Agra found his relations migrating to Pakistan and ultimately decided to leave the country. It was a difficult and much pain producing decision but there was no escape route. In many other stories and novels including Bhisham Sahani's *Tamas*, a Television serial, the trauma of partition with which Indians suffered has been dramatised. The effect of it on the Indian Muslims was that they retreated into a world of their own and tried to preserve their culture and religious ideology as interpreted by not very well educated Mullas. The community thereby instead of taking a progressive outlook fell prey to obscuration ideas and values. The worst sufferers of this situation were the Muslim women who were forced to embrace ignorance.

After Independence many laws were made to give equal rights to the Hindu women. The Hindu Code Bill conferred almost equal rights to women in the sphere of property and marriage etc. Unfortunately there has been complete absence of reform in Muslim family laws. The Indian constitution envisaged a single civil code for all the citizens of the country. But because a large section of the Muslims were extremely critical of a common civic code it could not be enacted. Muslims do not want that any changes be made in their personal law. But there are many provisions and interpretations of the Shariat, which go against the interests of the Muslim women. So while the Hindu society is on reformist trending the Muslim clergy favours the status quo. The outcome is that the women are sufferers. It may, however, be noted that there is no feminist movement worth the name sponsored by the Muslim women for the removal of any law that places them in an inferior position than men. The reason for this may be found in the Muslim women psyche. They have been so groomed that to raise any objection to the interpretation of the Shariat by the Ulemas is unthinkable. The restrictions on their education keep them perpetually in the sphere of ignorance.

The enactment of the Muslim Women's (Protection of Rights on Divorce) Bill in 1986 by the Indian Parliament was done because controversy arose over a case that came up for review in the Supreme Court. It is better known as Shah Bano's case. In this case the earlier judgment of the Supreme Court was that a husband was responsible of maintaining his wife. The orthodox argued against this judgment that is goes against the spirit of Shariat. A wife is entitled for her *Mehar* only. About this Bill Maitrayee Mukhopadhyay writes: "The Muslim Women's Bill constitutes a major attempt at codifying Muslim personal law, setting up boundaries delineating what Muslim women are entitled to in the event of a divorce. In the process Muslim women's entitlements have been redefined and men's responsibilities to their divorced "fixed" in a way that disempowers Muslim women".[1] It may be asserted that the Muslim women's fight for a fair treatment by their male counterparts faces very tough opposition in the name of keeping the separate identity of Muslims and in the name of not involving any other agency than what Ulemas consider as the right interpretation of religious texts.

Huma Ahmed-Ghosh writes: "The lifestyle, attitudes and cultural identity of Muslim women in India are an outcome of their socio-economic condition, and a tenuous relationship the Muslims share with the Hindus".[2] She in her article entitled "Preserving identity: a case study of Palitpur" examines the various indicators of the socio-economic status of Muslim women in Palitpur, a village in Meerut district, north India. She found the Muslim community in Palitpur as economically backward. But the economically depressed, Muslim men in Palitpur "Flaunted a moral and cultural superiority over the Hindus." In them there was a feeling that they belonged to the ruling (royal) class, (referring to the four-century rule of India by the Mughals). They felt that due to the creation of Pakistan they have been neglected or harassed by the government and Hindus because they stayed back.[2]

The above finding shows that the Muslims after partition ascribe to their backwardness the neglect by the government and blame the Hindus also. They have a sort of defeatist mentality. They want to keep their Islamic identity not by progressive education but by remaining rooted to the traditional education given in madrassas. In Palitpur there were only two schools, one the government school and the other the madrassa. Muslim children attended the madrassa that only imparted Islamic education. It is through such education that they wanted to keep their Muslim identity. In spite of this there was a sense of helplessness among them. They considered that their future was bleak.

The Muslim women in Palitpur were victims of "their gender as well as their minority status".[4] They were uneducated and conservative. In them the idea of good education was not at all inculcated. They considered the reason for their low socio-economic status lie in their victimisation by the Hindus and the neglect by the government. According to Ghosh : "Education which was the only way out,was still not encouraged. The sense of victimisation was very strong. For the women, conforming to Islamic tenets as rigidly as their socio-economic conditions would allow, was not only perceived as an improved lifestyle but also the onlv escape from their 'disadvantaged' situation".[5]

The case study of Palitpur may not be the representative of all the Muslims in India since there exists a diversity of culture and lifestyle among Muslims in different regions and states of India. But certainly it throws some light on the social status, aspirations and motivations of Muslim women of rural India. In Palitpur Muslim community aspires for upward mobility but not through learning or further understanding of the Quran, Hadith or Shariat. They try to achieve it by means of emulating the lifestyle of the Ashrafs, that is those who belong to higher social echelon.[6]

The Indian Muslim women's lower status and position is due to many factors. Some of these we have outlined above. The women are guided by the zeal resulting from their adherence to Islamic tenets as preached by male Muslim leaders. Many of their interpretations of the religious texts go against their interests but because of their ignorance and upbringing they are incapable of raising their voice against them. They also suffer from the feeling of helplessness for improving their lot. They are also fed with the propaganda that their plight is the result of a conspiracy by the Hindu fundamentalists which make them more rigid in the observance of the religious practies and the obedience of religious injections. The Mullahs and Muslim politicians have a stáke in keeping them backward and so they feed them with those notions that perpetuate their backwardness. The plight of Muslim women can improve only if they are encouraged to have liberal education and to think independently and assert their individuality.

REFERENCES

1. Maitrayee Mukhopadhyay,"Between Community and State: the question of women's rights and personal laws," in Zoya Hasan (edited). *Forging Identities, Gender, Communities and the State.* (edited). (New Delhi, 1994), p. 127.
2. Huma Ahmed-Ghosh, "Preserving Identity: A case study of Palitpur," in Zoya Hasan (edited), p. 169.
3. Huma Ahmed-Ghosh, p. 171.
4. *Ibid.*, p. 185.
5. *Ibid.*, p. 185.
6. *Ibid.*, p. 182.

11

STRESSES OF MODERN EDUCATED WOMEN

A modern educated women suffers from various tensions. If she is a housewife she feels stressed because her education has not incurred her any relief from domestic chores. If she is working woman she is stressed because of lack of co-ordination between her home and office life. This chapter identifies stresses typical to the modern educated woman and offers some suggestions for dealing with them.

The ambivalence that women feel as they take on dual roles of housewife and worker is quite tension producing. Undoubtedly, many women are able to combine both roles with smooth adjustments, particularly if the husband and the family members are co-operative and supportive. However, in many families, the conflict between both the roles has created estrangement between either the husband or the wife or the wife and the other members of the family.

We have in the previous chapters traced the psychology of the Indian women in terms of her desire for domination and her will for subordination. The large number of women who have traditional outlook are meeting with their tensions and stresses by overtly subordinating themselves to men and covertly trying to dominate them by their extreme devotion and sense of duty. The modern emancipated women are revolting against this duplicity. They are denying the superiority of the male and seeking an equality between the sexes overtly and covertly both. We have also advocated that through our educational system the women should learn to move towards equality of sexes without involving themselves in any duplicity in their behaviour pattern. But the danger in such a move is the enhancement of tensions and stresses in the individuals, in the families and also in the society.

Ambitious men of lower income group want their wives and daughters to work and earn to help raise the family's standard of living. At the same time these men cannot tolerate the idea of independence such as that they themselves have on the job. They are unable to free themselves from the myths of Sita and Savitri.They become agitated when their women become assertive and begin to express their personal views and opinions and their likes and dislikes. They feel that women are transgressing their freedom, which they have so generously bestowed on them. Their ego is hurt if their wife's income exceeds their own income. But the women when they go out for work cannot be bound in the chains of orthodoxy. Hence the modern woman's tensions enhance as she has to cope with the demands of her job and the dictates of her male relations.

In a study by Mukta Mittal on "Educated Women Power," it was found that the need for supplementing the family income was the chief motivating factor for encouraging the respondents belonging to "lowly educated" and "moderately educated" groups to become job seekers and get themselves registered at the Employment Exchange Bureaus. But in the case of "highly educated" respondents, the prime motivating factor behind encouraging them in their becoming registrants for job was "desire to be free from dependence on family members and relatives".[1]

Many conflicts arise when both husband and wife are working. The husband desires that the wife should take up job but disapproves the complete involvement of the wife in the job For him the job of the wife is only a secondary commitment. Her primary duty he feels is towards him and his family. He wants his wife to work and also to take up full time duties of looking after the household. When the wife is unable to cope with this situation the seeds of conflict and estrangement between the husband and wife begin to germinate. After returning from her work the wife is tired but she receives no sympathy or help from her husband or in-laws. When the tensions so created become unbearable the wife has no option but to resign from the job. But this is also not liked by the husband who resents the loss of income and blames the wife for not being able to reconcile between her job outside and her duties to her family.

The tension reduction in such cases is possible when all the family members recognise that the household work is to be shared and is a joint responsibility of all the members of the family. In those families in which the joint responsibiliy is recognised the tensions are suitably dealt with.

Till nearly three decades earlier the women were giving utmost importance to the role of the housewife. In a study by Cora Vreede Stuer in 1970 it was reported that quite a substantial number of girls "consider the role of the housewife as the most suitable." But when they were asked that if they had to go outside the home to work, most of them said they would prefer to teach or do social work.[2] One girl in Cora's study remarked: "I would be willing to work in my field, but if my husband opposed it, I would submit to his wishes." Similar views were expressed by 18 of 15 educated women in Rama Mehta's study of the Western Educated Hindu women in 1970. One woman in her study expressed this view : "Working was not important enough for me to go against my husband's wishes. After marriage, one cannot do as one wants; working is not an important enough issue to create tensions".[3] It may be noted that till seventies or may be later also the working women, generally, perceived their main role as that of wife or mother. By such an attitude they were meeting with their tensions created by their becoming working women. But the situation at the end of the twentieth century is not as simple as that. The aspirations and the motivations of the women have increased manifolds and so also there is increase in their stresses and tensions.

Society now has a more favourable attitude towards the employment of women in the middle income groups. It has become an economic need. Promilla Kapur in her study in seventies took a sample of 300 working women from three major occupations teachers, office workers and doctors. She observed that because of society's change of attitude, as well as change in attitudes of the educated married women towards their own employment, their number has multiplied to the extent that they now constitute a class by themselves. This class is facing the greatest change and challenge ever offered anywhere in the world to the feminine population.[4]

The number of women seeking jobs has increased manifolds now from that of seventies. The challenges before them have also become quite serious. The educated women have first to face the spectre of unemployment. The job market is very tight. It is difficult for men to get the jobs and when women also compete with them the number of the job seekers becomes quite high. With the limited job opportunities the women also suffer from the various types of restrictions which are put on them by the society. They still search the jobs, which are considered feminine in nature like the teaching, or nursing or office work, etc.They also want a job in the town or place to which they belong. They do not opt for the jobs in the villages or remote areas. It is not only due to the intention of the women that they do not want to work at the distant places from their homes but also due to the living conditions. It is difficult for a single working woman to find a decent living place in most of the towns or big cities. The security environment in the country is also not such as the women may move very freely. The cases of eve teasing are on the increase and the single working woman becomes an easy prey of unscrupulous males.

The women's problems are three-fold with regard to getting employment. First of all, they have to compete in an overcrowded job market. Secondly, their families and society do not allow them to serve in those professions, which are branded as predominantly masculine in nature, even though there may be no restriction from the side of the employing authorities. Thirdly, they have the problem of finding suitable living accommodation if they get a job away from their homes or native place and added to this is the problem of security for a single working woman. All these problems are stress producing in the educated women. But it may be said that the stresses of the women can be reduced if they themselves and the society approach towards the solution of the problems with some dedication. There is no doubt in it that the number of jobs has to be increased. More efforts should be made to educate the women to generate self-employment. They may also be given vocational training. A change is to be brought in their own attitudes and the attitudes of the society and the family that it is a myth that the women are incapable of taking up some jobs which are masculine in nature. The women are capable of taking up all those jobs, which are considered masculine. In Chapter 7 we have forcefully built the case of sexual equality on the basis of the physiology of the male and the female. Lastly, the government and the society must come forward to build "Working Women's Homes." In some towns they have been built. The need is to have a chain of such homes in each town and township.

There is another type of conflict with which the working women suffer. This is in relation to their work environment. The working women rightly demand that they should be accepted and respected as equally capable and efficient workers as males. The conflict occurs when they simultaneously demand special privileges and advantages because they are the women and the weaker sex. For example, they take up jobs that require night duties but after taking the job they may claim that since they are ladies they may be exempted from working in the night. They may press the employer to transfer them to some daytime job and transfer some male to this job. This becomes a conflict-producing situation. Some women also shirk work claiming that they are women and so entitled for light work. To avoid such conflicts the women need to develop professional attitude. There are many examples of successful women.

There is another side of the picture as well. The men resent the working women in their midst. In an office in which men and women both work the men do not feel as free with the women as with their men colleagues. If male becomes too intimate gossips are unleashed. If he ignores them he is branded as the chauvinistic male. There seems to be a need to develop a code of ethics for interpersonal relationships in those situations in which the males and females have to work in close co-ordination.

A very serious situation is developing in some places of work where the boss is male and he tries to sexually exploit his female employees. The women organizations, the government and even the courts are seized with this problem. Some women take the courage to make complaints about this behaviour of their officers or male colleague but there are lots of women who silently suffer at the hands of office sharks. Sometimes men also become victims of women's manipulations.They make false complaints about their exploitation so that the persons concerned are defamed. It is because of this danger that the complaints of women regarding exploitation are being scrutinized cautiously. Such situations can be avoided in case men and women both are made to realise that there shall be no discrimination in the work situations on the basis of sex. Both men and women must view each other as equal partners in work performance and must expect that recognition shall depend on their efficiency and quality of work and not on their sex.

As has already been pointed out that greatest danger resulting from a woman being career oriented is disharmony within her family. In Kapur's study of much marital maladjustment, the husband expected the wife to work as well as serve him and the household. The husbands generally believed in absolute supremacy over their wives and desired complete surrender and devotion from them. Those women who asserted their individuality were severely punished and ruthlessly treated, In cases where women could not tolerate the brutalities, they were separated from their spouses.[5]

If the husband demands that his wife quit work and she refuses it creates much tension in the family. In those cases in which the husband is transferred and the wife refuses to quit her job and go with him, legal problems arise.The husband may sue his wife for the restoration of conjugal rights. In such cases the attitude of the Indian courts has not been very decisive. Kusum (1976) cited many cases in which the wife was asked to leave her job and join her husband. In one case (Gaya Prasad Vs. Smt. Bhagwati) in Madhya Pradesh, the wife worked as *Gram Sevika* due to financial circumstances. The husband petitioned for the restitution of conjugal rights. The observations of the court while delivering the judgement were: "Merely on the ground that the husband has a small income, and the wife if allowed to serve at a place away from the marital home, can substantially augment the family, cannot be held to be a sufficient reason to deny the wife's society to the husband".[6]

The above judgement was given in the sixties. From seventies onwards the change in the attitudes of the courts is noticeable, as judgements have become much less traditional. The judges concede that in case of genuine economic necessity, the wife has a right to maintain her job. But the main problem here is not only the economic necessity but also a woman's freedom to take her own decisions. The woman's personal satisfaction, sense of confidence and security and her intellectual needs must be the guiding factors in making a decision about her quitting the job or remaining in service while living away from her husband or family. Whatever may be the decisions of the courts the stressful life between the husband or and wife will continue to be lived till there is the recognition that wife also has aspirations, ambitions and a will of her own. The idea that the women should work only to supplement their husbands incomes is to give them much inferior position in the family than that of husbands and of considering them as only the instruments for augmenting the family incomes. The women should not be viewed as the objects or instruments, but as entities unto themselves.

Narrow and conservative concepts of in-laws are also tension producing. The in-laws, in many cases want that their daughters-in-law take up jobs but at the same time are extremely critical if she is late in returning from her place of work or is not above to do the household work as efficiently as they expect her to do.

Some studies indicate that women seek work equal to the level of their husband's prestige. In case a wife is not equally educated or trained she may prefer to stay at home rather than accept work below her husband's level. In such a case if she is forced to undertake inferior status work she remains tense and suffers from inferiority complex. The woman herself can take steps to come out of such situation by undertaking courses or training to improve her qualifications.

There is another side of the picture also. If the wife is employed in a job which has higher prestige and emoluments than the husband's job, the husband feels jealous and threatened. In many cases the tension between the husband and wife becomes so intense that living under the same roof becomes a torture leading to divorce or separation or to perpetual quarrels between them. There can develop proper amity and understanding between them if the wife tries to understand the sentiments of the husband and the husband realises that his wife deserves what she is getting. Truly well adjusted couples are those who respect each others individuality. A husband and wife can achieve harmony through mutual support and self-esteem. When both work role differentiation should not exist. The husband should give full emotional support to the wife and the wife should be considerate to the needs of the husband, may they be either psychological, physical, sexual or economical.

The girls including those who are educated find it very difficult to get a husband who does not demand dowry. In fact now the eligible bachelors and their families are demanding that the girls be educated so that they can earn money and also a dowry to meet the initial expenses of setting the home. The dowry demands are increasing day by day with the rising ambitions for equipping the houses with the modern gadgets. The eductaed girls whose parents search bridegrooms who are well-employed and highly educated face demands of exorbitant amounts as dowries. Such demands many parents are not able to meet with. The sensitive girls feel themselves as the cause of their parent's woes and blame themselves for being born as girls. Sometimes their tensions increase so much that they even commit suicide.

The statistics relating to dowry are very grim. Sometime back it was announced in the Lok Sabha that as many as 878 cases of dowry murders and 1,479 cases of dowry suicides were registered in the country in 1990. The educated girls who resent their husband's and in-laws demands of dowry are brutally killed or forced to commit suicide. In order to stop these great human tragedies and combat horrible social evils, it would be necessary to bring about radical transformation, in the old rigid social structure. The parents of the educated girls rear them up in such a rigid environment that they themselves are incapable of finding their own life partners. They have to depend on the traditional system of marriage. The educated girls may be saved from much stress if they are left free to make a choice of their own mates. The rigid social structure can be changed only when a brave new philosophy of life steeped in socio-economic and moral values of equality of all castes and both the sexes is evolved out and adopted. Such a philosohpy will enable the male as well as the female child to spontaneously internalise the principle of equality of man, woman of all castes and creeds.

The Indian women are marching ahead in each and every field of work and activity. They are in the forefront of all the movements for progress and development. But unfortunately the area of social reforms, which touches them directly, is as yet a neglected area. The movement for women emancipation and empowerment are ridiculed and made fun of by the traditionally oriented males. The women have little say in the Parliament or state legislatures because their number is extremely limited in these bodies. The Bill for 30 per cent reservation of seats for women in the Parliament is opposed on one flimsy ground or another Our Parliament and legislatures are responsible for the governance and the administration of the country. On them are needed such persons who are highly motivated towards efficient management, adequately educated, well-informed and possess a zeal for social service. The country at present has quite a substantial number of such women who can adorn the seats of the Parliament. There are, however, some leaders who want those women in the Parliament who are mere appendages of their husbands or male relatives. The ridiculous thing is that they want to do it in the name of social justice.

The stresses and the tensions of the modern educated Indian women can be minimised if they involve themselves in a strong movement of women emancipation and empowerment. In the Indian context it means the deliverance from the myths which have been woven around them and the false pedestal at which they have been put since long.

In 1963 Frieden wrote: *The Feminine Mystique* which attempted to explode many myths about women. Her thesis is applicable to both East and West. She writes—"the Victorian culture did not permit women to accept or gratify their basic sexual needs, our culture does not permit women to accept or gratify their basic need to grow and fulfill their potentialities as human beings, a need which is not solely defined by their sexual role".[7] Just as the Indian women have been led to believe that their fulfillment lies in motherhood and wifely duties, so Friedan observes about American women: "In the feminine mystique, there is no other way she can even dream about herself, except as her children's mother, her husband's wife."[8]

Simone de Beauvoir considers that the myth of feminine 'mystery' has several advantages for the male. He can dismiss inexplicable moods, behaviours, and feelings by saying :"Oh Women! Who can understand them any way?"[9] Rohrbaugh Joanna adds: "Since woman cannot be understood, man cannot be expected to build an authentic relationship with her. He is free to relate to her in terms of his own perceptions, fantasies and desires".[10]

Williams referring to the myth of woman as mystery says : "By defining her as mysterious other, man spares himself the necessity of analysing her behaviours and understanding it as a consequence of her position vis-a-vis him. To do that would require acknowledgement of her oppression, and a possible shift in their power relationship? The price would be very high".[11]

In such a 'mystique' or lifestyle, a woman's intelligence has no meaning and her capability is negated. By following a monotonous daily routine, she loses all interest in the outside world, draws herself into a shell and spends her time in gossips. She is little more than an instrument, which keeps a constant supply of members through her powers of reproduction.

Friedan emphasises that one's individuality when becoming a wife and mother should not be given up, but strengthened. She says: "Maslow found that the individuality is strengthened, that the ego is in one sense merged with another, but yet in another sense remains separate, and strong as always. The two tendencies, to transceud individuality and to sharpen and strengthen it, must be seen as partners and not as contradictory"[12]. Self-actualised educated women should serve their society and contribute their best to humanity, just as men have the opportunity to do so. The world has suffered enough because half of humanity has remained dependent on the other half.

Indian women are often viewed as passive, prudish and fragile. Many of them feel that a mere lustful glance or touch by a non-relative male leads to the loss of their chastity. The women's movements should actively try to alter such a nonsensical perception. It may be remembered that the women in general and the educated women in particular are in danger of becoming not only household slaves but also work place slaves if they do not learn to become individualistic and assertive.

An Indian woman with lustre, with a brilliance of her won, with a dynamic attitude towards life and with the charm of a sturdy woman going about her business is always in danger of being branded as aggressive, too outgoing and, perhaps, flirtatious, This type of woman is incongruent with the image of the ideal that has been imprinted on the minds of the Indians for the centuries, The women's movements should be in the direction of relieving intelligent, modern women from the clutches of orthodoxy. The real women's movement which India need and towards which the Indian feminists seem to be fully conscious is that of removal of orthodoxy, blind faith, poverty, helplessness, dependence and complete subjugation of woman's will. The reformers should try to bring the changes in the attitudes of both male and female regarding marriage and the family. The must attack fanatical religious rites, ill conceived notions of virginity, wrong notions of chastity, custom of giving or taking dowry, wastage in the marriage ceremonies and similar other outdated customs and traditions.

We may agree with Carden when he says that : "The new feminism is not about the elimination of differences between the sexes, nor even simply the achievement of equal opportunity; it concerns with the individual's right to find out the kind of person he or she is and to strive to become that person".[13]

REFERENCES

1. Mukta Mittal, "Educated Women Power." In Mukta Mittal (ed.) (New Delhi, 1995).
2. Cora Vreede de Stuers, *Girl Students in Jaipur*, (New York, 1970), p. 116.
3. Rama Mehta, *The Western Educated Hindu Women*, (New York, 1970), p. 40.
4. Promilla Kapur, *Marriage and the Working Women in India*, (Delhi, 1972), p. 5.

5. Promilla Kapur, pp. 13-150.
6. Kusum, "Can wife be made to give up job?" in *The Hindustan Times Weekly*, (Sunday, Jan. 4. 1976).
7. Betty Frieden, *The Feminine Mystique*, (New York, 1963), p. 77.
8. Betty Friedan, p. 62.
9. Simone de Beauvoir, Quoted in hoanna Bunker Rohrbaugh. *Women Psychology's Puzzle*, (New York, 1979), p. 5.
10. Joanna Bunker Rohrbaugh, p. 5.
11. J.H. Williams, *Psychology of Women: Behavior in a Bio Social Context*, (New Yoɪk, 1977), p. 7.
12. Betty Friedan, pp. 323-324.
13. Maren Lockwood Carden. *The New Feminist Movement*, (New York, 1974), p. 10.

12

FUTURISTIC TRENDS IN WOMEN EDUCATION

India is a developing country, which depends very much on its vast potential of human resources, If these resources are properly tapped the country is bound to progress efficiently, effectively and rapidly. Women form the most important part of the human resources of the nation and they may contribute very substantially in building a strong, powerful and affluent nation. They can, however, make their best contribution when they are properly educated and are able to explode the myths, which have kept them in a state of backwardness and neglect. In the present chapter we are trying to project the type of education which is needed in future for Indian women in view of their socio-phychological make up.

Today too much theory based on little reality exists. Men talk of morality while all the time degrading their women. The reformists talk of abstinence to reduce population while they themselves might have fathered more than half a dozen children. The harmony in family life is preached while subjugating the women in the name of old ideal of *Pativrata*. The quarrels between the husband and wife may involve much cruelty yet the divorce may be very much condemned. There is an urgent need to cry a half to this type of duplicity in talks and action. For example, when there is genuine discord between husband

and wife or there is much cruelty involved in their relationship then divorce is the only viable solution. It will injure the ego of the children much less than their upbringing in a daily quarrelsome situation. But this point of no return in the relationship between husband and wife will not come up if both respect each other's individuality and live together with mutual trust, faith, desire and love. In a stable marriage alliance consideration of each other's viewpoint is desirable and Indian men and women have the capability of developing such consideration.

There is enough scientific evidence available, which shows that since birth onwards girl child receives rejection, unequal, indifferent and discriminatory treatment as compared to male children. Access to food and other household assets, allocation of domestic duties, participation in community and neighbourhood activities, school education, etc. reflect serious gender based differences and inequalities.[1]

Modern scientific techniques like amniocentesis and ultrasound have been widely misused as "sex determination test"for selective elimination of the female foetuses. Between 1978 and 1983, 78,000 female were aborted in India, following sex determination tests. A Mumbai-based survey in 1984 revealed that out of the 8,000 foetuses aborted following such tests 7,999 were female. Many State Governments have framed or are framing legislation against this practice. But still there is a danger that secretly such tests will continue to be conducted and femal foetuses aborted. The tradition of having a male child is so deep-rooted that the women themselves do not hesitate in destroying their pregnancies if the tests reveal that the baby to be born is a female. Proper education is needed to discourage this tendency. It has been noticed that many educated women also indulge in the practice of destroying foetuses hence our emphasis is on proper education by which we mean an education, which frees the woman from gender biases.

Conservative cultural values, coupled with assumption of demestic responsibilities dictate the girl child's withdrawal from formal education. In our country the female literacy rates are very low. These are 39.4 per cent according to the 1991 census. The drop out rate for girls in the school is estimated at 55.5 per cent at the primary stage and 77.7 per cent at the middle school stage.[2] There is thus great need for having a crash programme for women education.

It is unfortunate that in spite of Indian women getting all those legal rights which are being demanded by the women of some developed nations they are having quite difficult time in freeing themselves from the old fossilised traditions. The mother cult may be one of the reasons for their remaining tradition oriented. Though that which is motherly is represented as noble, it has its drawbacks as well in those situations in which the women cannot think of any other thing except being mothers. The motherhood syndrome is incompatible with modern woman's development and exists because of cultural conditioning. According to Evelyn Reed: "The subordination of the women is not the result of a predetermined biological handicap. i.e. child bearing." She considers that attribution of inferior status of women to her faulty biology is a false preposition.[3]

Self-reliance, self-esteem and a reality-oriented approach to life must be the goal of Indian women. Some people may take exception to this suggestion because of the fear of loss of domestic harmony but unless the women are able to assert their will the family and the social life will remain in a state of disharmony.

Futuristic Trends in Women Education

After independence India framed planning, strategies and techniques to steer the nation's economic development towards attaining a socialist pattern of society. The first five-year plan was launched in 1950-51 and thereafter nine more five-year plans besides some yearly plans have already been adopted. In each of these plans women's development issues, especially their economic, educational and health issues, have reveived considerable attention and various welfare measures were taken to ameliorate their conditions. The result of all these measures is that the status and position of the Indian women have much improved. But as we have repeated again and again in this book there is much, which has still to be done.

The Draft of the National Policy on Empowerment of Women released by the Ministry of Human Resource Development seeks to eliminate all forms of violence against women as also to abolish discrimination against the girl child. It commits the government to ensure that women are not denied of their human rights and fundamental freedoms. This policy also seeks to provide equal opportunities for power sharing and decision-making to women at all levels and processes in public and private sectors. All these are highly desirable goals. But these alone would not be sufficient unless the government policies and its mechanism are supplemented by a social will, a wave and a movement by women themselves for achieving these goals and for promoting rational attitudinal changes.

The National Policy on Education (NPE) 1986 has given very important recommendations for women education. It has paid attention to the basic issues of women's equality. In the section titled '*Education for Women's Equality*' the Policy states :

> "Education will be used as an agent of basic change in the status of women. In order to neutralise the accumulated distortions of the past, these will be a well-conceived edge in favour of women. The national education system will pay a positive role in the empowerment of women. It will foster the development of new values through redesigned curricula textbooks, training and orientation of teachers, decision makers and administrators, and the active involvement of educational institutions---- women's studies will be promoted as a part of various courses and educational institutions encouraged to take up active programmes to further women's development.

The removal of women's illiteracy and obstacles inhibiting their access to, and retention in, elementary education will receive overriding priority, through provision of special support services, setting of time targets and effective monitoring. Major emphasis will be laid on women's participation in vocational, technical and professional education at different levels. The policy of non-discrimination will be pursued vigorously to eliminate sex stereotyping in vocational and professional courses and to promote women's participation in non-traditional ocupation, as well as in emisting and exerged technologies".[4]

The above recommendations have given very important guidelines for the futuristic education of the women. The government definitely took interest in implementing the policy framework and so there were developed "Programme of Action" in 1986 and 1992. Also a National Perspective Plan for Women's Education 1997-98 to 2000 AD. was drawn. The National Perspective Plan formulated some important specific objectives for women education so that women may also participate actively in the social, cultural, economic and political areas. These important objectives were to be obtained by 2000 AD. These objectives included elimination of illiteracy and universalisation of elementary education, substantial vocalisation and diversification of courses at secondary level, making education as an effective means for women equality, making necessary intervention in the content and processes of education to inculcate positive and egalitarian attitudes, providing non-formal and part-time courses to women to enable them to acquire knowledge and skills for their social, cultural and economic advancement, and to provide impetus to women to enroll themselves in various professional degree courses so as to increase their number in medicine, teaching, engineering and other fields substantially. To achieve the above mentioned and some other objectives the National Perspective Plan made important recommendations that awareness needs to be generated among the masses regarding the necessity of educating girls so as to prepare them to effectively contribute to the socio-economic development of the country, to strengthen their role in society and to realise their own capacities for improving and minimising drop-outs and wastage of girl students.

The Revised Plan of Action (1992) has laid down suitable strategies for implementing the above mentioned targets.

In spite of all endeavours made so far for promoting women education, we still find that for every 100 boys there are only 62 girls in primary schools, 43 girls in middle schools, 36 girls in secondary schools and 31 girls at different stages of higher education. According to the 1991 census female literacy is 39.4 per cent compared to 63.8 per cent for males, the total number of female illiterates is 197 millions which is more than male counterparts by 70 millions, even though the female population is less than the male population by 32 millions. There are rural urban disparities and among women, rural female literacy is about half of the urban female literacy.[5]

The above figures lead us to conclude that more intensive efforts are needed to educate our women specially those who are living in the rural areas or the slum areas in the towns. Since most of these women who are illiterate and do not go to the school the programmes for educating them may be accompanied with the programmes of improving their financial conditions. The programmes for the poverty alleviation should be intensified. It may be emphasised that the success of any scheme of education depends to a great extent on it being productive both in the material as well as social sense. Actually education should lead to social, economic and moral development. An educated person must be able to earn more than an uneducated one. The national education system will play a positive, interventionist role in the empowerment of women. It will foster the development of new values through redesigned curricula, textbooks, training and orientation of teachers, decision-makers and administrators, and the active involvement of educational instititutions. Women's studies will be promoted as a part of various courses and educational instutions. Women's studies will be promoted as a part of various courses and educational institutions encouraged taking up active programmes to further women's development.

The removal of women's illiteracy and obstacles

inhibiting their access to, and retention in, elementary education will receive overriding priority, through provision of special support services, setting of time targets and effective monitoring. Major emphasis will be laid on women's participation in vocational, technical and professional education at different levels. The policy of non-discrimination will be pursued vigorously to eliminate sex stereo-typing in vocational and professional courses and to promote women's contribution effectively towards bringing desirable social change and be honest, sincere and affectionate individual. For our women such education is required which may help them in getting gainful employment and in improving their financial position.

From the above discussion it may be evident that the government is very much aware of the need of providing education to the women of the country. In the recent decades it has made some genuine efforts to bring the women on the national scene by giving them incentives, providing for their education schools and colleges, giving free education to the girls up to a particular stage, developing centres of women studies, opening various avenues of employment to them, providing non-formal centres for their vocational training. It is very much desirable that no discrimination is made on the basis of jobs meant exclusively for males or for females. The interest of the student should be the main consideration. From the lower classes onwards the attention of the students should be directed towards creating social awareness and motivating them for higher achievements in all the areas of concern to them. India needs good housewives as well as efficient women workers. Education for women must be organised around these two powerful needs.

It is to be noted that the outlook of the women has changed considerably during the last four decades. Much of it is due to the expansion of education that has taken place in the country. The young women of today are neither afraid of moving out of their homes nor are as dependent on their parents or husbands as were their mothers and grand mothers. The woman wants to be economically independent. She has realised the importance of education and is quite conscious of the need of raising the standard of living of the family through her engagement in the world of work. The educated women are prepared to fight for their rights and to assert their individuality. Hence web may say that the educational efforts made so far have yielded positive results. These efforts are now required to be intensified.Certain changes in the educational system are also needed so that the women learn to be self-reliant, are able to develop self-esteem and become caring, loving and the source of amity and goodwill in the family. The following are some suggestions regarding the changes to be brought about in the educational system:

1. All out efforts should be made to implement the constitutional directives of compulsory elementary education up to 14 years of age. Education should be free up to this age for both boys and girls.

2. The girls should be taught the same subjects as are being taught to the boys, which means that if home craft is taught to the girls it should also be taught to the boys. The physical education should be given to both boys and girls. At the onset of puberty the girl's menses begin. At this age some training in personal hygiene may be given exclusively to the girls.

3. From the lower classes onwards the attention of the students should be directed towards social evils and in them social awareness should be created. They should also be motivated for higher achievements in all the areas of concern to them. As said earlier India needs good housewives as well as efficient women workers. Education for women must be organised around these two powerful needs.

4. The girls should be encouraged to join technical, managerial, professional institutions of higher learning so that they can compete with boys in the job market.

5. The methods of teaching should be so planned that they inculcate the habits of thinking freely and expressing their views freely.

6. The curricula of all the subjects, which are taught to the school children, should be free from sex bias.

7. The education of the school children must include co-curricular activities in which both boys and girls should participate and learn to take independent decisions.

8. In our educational institutions the courses in the maintenance of inter-personal relationships be introduced. Some of these courses must be compulsory for both boys and girls.

9. Some special courses for girls in mother craft, in the home economics and household affairs should be introduced. Some of such courses may also be open for boys.

10. Non-formal system of education must be strengthened. It should be available to all those girls who are unable to join the formal system of education. Education from the elementary to postgraduate levels must be available through this system.

11. A network of adult literacy centres must be established throughout the country. In these centres the education for social change must be stressed. The women must specially be prepared to fight against social evils and to rise above their mythical existence.

12. A network of counselling centres must be set up. These centres must be equipped with to give educational, vocational and personal counselling. Special emphasis should also be placed to marigal and family conselling. Each big school must have adequately trained counsellors. Counselling is very much needed at the adolescent stage to both the boys and girls. Our educational system must be able to fulfil this need.

13. Precaution should be taken in teaching those topics, which involve the status and position of women. It will all depend on the teachers how they present an episode where the women are depicted as serving their husbands. It may be taught in terms of inferior position of the women or it may be taught as an ideal example of love and affection. The teachers training colleges or colleges of education

should pay special attention towards the teaching of such lessons by their teacher trainees so that the myths regarding women perpetuated in our society for centuries are exploded and the modern outlook is inculcated.

14. The educational institutions must also provide placement services so that the boys and girls are not only prepared for jobs but are also able to be placed in jobs.

15. The emphasis on the education of the girls must be specifically on making them strong so that they are able to reverse their image of being delicate and unfit for jobs requiring tough exterior.

The above are some of the suggestions which have emerged out of the discussions made in the different chapters of the present book. Many useful and worthwhile suggestions have been made by various commissions and committees, plans and policies. We have refrained ourselves form repeating them, as they are available in the from of reports in full details. In planning or the futuristic education they may all be taken into consideration?

In conclusion we may say that the Indian women have always been quite strong. They have always been in the forefront of the struggle for the betterment of the mankind. They have been great support to their male counterpart. It is their power of resilience that in spite of the persistent efforts of the male to enmesh them in the web of myth they have never lost their composure and cool and today they are bravely facing the challenges of their subjugation.

REFERENCES

1. Mukta Mittal, "Girl child: A neglected dimension in India," in Mukta Mittal (ed.) *Women in India: Today and Tomorrow*, (New Delhi, 1995), p. 108.
2. Usha Batra, "Psycho-social and Philosophical Dimensions of Women Education in India and the Projection of Futuristic Trends: A Theoretical Study," *Unpublished Ph.D. thesis* submitted to Panjab University (Chandigarh, 1997), p. 155.

3. E. Reid, *Women Evolution from Matriarchal Clan to Patriarchal Family*, (New York, 1977), p. 44.
4. *The National Policy of Education*, (New Delhi, 1986).
5. Usha Batra, *Unpublished Ph. D. Thesis.*

BIBLIOGRAPHY

Agrawal, Usha: *Indian Women Education and Development*, Ambala: The Indian Publications, 1995.

Aruna, Asaf Ali: "Women's Suffrage in India," *Our Cause*, edited Shyam Kumari Nehru, Allahabad, Kitabistan, 1937.

Altekar, A.S.: *The Position of Women in Hindu Civilization*, Delhi: Motilal Banarsidas, 1962.

Arora, K.K. *et. al*: "Women and Career," *Group Project Report*, Bombay, Tata Institute of Social Sciences, 1963.

Badel, Auguste: *Women: Past, Present and Future*, New York, Bone and Liveright, 1918.

Bader, Clarisse: *Women in Ancient India*, Delhi: Anmol Publications, 1987.

Baig Tara Ali: *India's Woman Position*, Delhi: S. Chand and Company Pvt. Ltd., 1976.

Bala, Usha: *Indian Women Freedom Fighters*, New Delhi: Manohar Publication, 1986.

Barot, Jyoti: "Modern trends in marital relations," *The Indian Family in the Change and Challenge of the Seventies*, New Delhi: Sterling Publishers, 1972.

Bebel, August: *Women in the Past, Present and Future*, ed. By Mukerjee, Subrata and Rama Swami, Sushila, New Delhi: Deep and Deep Publication, 1996.

Bhushan, Jamila Brij: "The Unassertive Sex," *The Hindustan Times*, Jan. 11, 1976.

Bhushan, Jamila Brij: *Muslim Women*, New Delhi: Vikas Publishing House, 1980.

Billington, Mary Frances: *Women in India*, Delhi: Amarka Book Agency, 1973.

Bose, Moni Mohan: *Female Education in India*, Kanpur, B.B. Gupta Publication, 1921.

Carden, Maren Lockwood: *The New Feminist Movement*, N.Y. Russall Sage Foundation, 1974.

Carstairs, G. Morris: *The Twice Born*, Bloomington: Indiana University Press, 1958.

Carstairs, G. Morris: "Village Women of Rajasthan," in *Indian Women*, ed. by Devaki Jain, New Delhi: Pub. Div., Ministry of Information and Broadcasting, Govt. of India, 1975.

Chakrapani, C, Kumar S. Vijaya (editors): *Changing Status and Role of Women in Indian Society*, New Delhi, M.D. Pub., 1994.

Chattapadhya, Kamladevi, *et. al*: *The Awakening of Indian Women*, Madras: Everyman's Press, 1939.

Cormack, Margaret: *The Hindu Women*, Bombay: Asia Pub. House, 1961.

Cousins, Margaret E.: *Towards Progress and Freedom*, Madras: Everyman's Press, 1939.

Das, Ram Mohan: *Women in Manu's Philosophy*, Jalandhar, ASB Pub., 1993.

Desai Devangana: *Erotic Sculpture of India: A Socio-Cultural Study*, New Delhi: Tata McGraw Pub., 1975.

Desai, Neera and Patel Vibbuti: *Indian Women*, Bombay: Popular Prakashan, 1975-85.

De'Souza Alfred: *Women in Contemporary India and South Asia*, Delhi: Manohar Pub., 1980.

Devasia, L. and Devasia, V.V: *Empowering Women for Sustainable Development*, New Delhi: Ashish Pub. House, 1994.

Dubey, S.C: "Men's and Women's Role in India: a Sociological Review," in *Women in the New Asia*, ed. by Barbara Ward, Paris: UNESCO, 1968.

Engineer Asghar Ali: *Islam and Liberation Theology*, New Delhi: Sterling Pub., 1990.

Everett, J.M.: *Women and Social Change in India*, Heritage Pub., 1979.

Friedan, Betty: *The Feminine Mystique*, N.Y., W.W. Norton, 1963.

Gandhi, M.K.: *The Role of Women*, Bombay: Bhartiya Vidhya Bhavan, 1964.

Ghadially, Rehana: *Women in Indian Society*, New Delhi: Sage Pub 1988.

Goldstein, Rhoda L.: *Indian Women in Transition: A Banglore Case Study*, New Jersey: The Scarecrow Press Inc., 1972.

Government of India: *Fourth World Conference on Women, Beijing 1995, Country report*, Deptt. of Women and Child Development, Ministry of Human Resource Development, New Delhi, 1995.

Gupta, A.K.: *Women and Society*, New Delhi: Criterion Pub., 1986.

Gupta, A.R.: *Women in Hindu Society*, Delhi: Jyotsna Prakashan, 1982.

Gupta, A.R.: *Women and Society*, Delhi: Criterion Pub., 1985.

Gupta, J.L.: *Challenges to the Fair Sex*, Delhi: Gyan Pub., 1988.

Hasan, Zoya (ed.): *Forging Identities, Gender, Communities and the State*, New Delhi: Kali for Women, 1994.

Gullahorn, J.E.: *Psychology and Women in Transition*, New York: John Wiley, 1979.

Hate, C.A.: *Hindu Women and her Future*, Bombay: New Bombay Co.,1948.

Hornel, I.B.: *Women in Early Buddhist Literature*, Kandy: Buddhist Publication Society, 1961.

Horney, Karen: *Feminine Psychology*, N.Y.: W.W. Norton & Co., 1967.

Indra Prof: *The Status of Women in Ancient India*, Lahore: The Minerva Book Shop, 1940.

Jain, D: *Indian Women*, Delhi: Publication Division, Government of India, 1975.

Jain, P.C., Jain, Shashi and Bhatnagar, Sudha (eds.): *Scheduled Caste Women*, Jaipur: Rawat Pub., 1997.

Jain, Pratibha and Mahan, Rajan: *Women Images*, Jaipur: Rawat Pub., 1996.

Jayal, Shakambari: *The Status of Women in Epics*, Delhi: Motilal Banarsidas, 1966.

Jayashree: *India and Indian Women*, Aligarh: Granthayan, 1980.

Jogdand, P.G. (ed.): *Dalit Women, Issues and Perspectives*, New Delhi: Gyan Publishing House, 1995.

Kalarani: *Role Conflict in Working Women*, New Delhi: Chitra Pub., 1976.

Kapur, Promilla: *The Changing Status of the Working Woman in India*, Delhi: Vikas Pub., 1974.

Kapur, Promilla: *Marriage and the Working Woman in India*, Delhi: Vikas Pub., 1975.

Kaur, Inderjeet: *Status of Hindu Women in India*, Allahabad: Chugh Pub., 1985.

Keeton Kathy and Basrin Yvonne: *Woman of Tomorrow*, N.Y.: Harvard Univ. Press, 1985.

Khanna, G: *Indian Women Today*, New Delhi: Publishing House, 1978.

Kidwai, Shaikh M.H.: *Women under Different Social and Religious Law*, New Delhi: Seema Pub., 1976.

Kirpal, Viney (ed.): *The Girl Child in 20th Century Indian Literature*, New Delhi: Sterling Pub., 1992.

Kishwar Madhu: *Off the Beaten Track, Rethinking Gender Justice for Indian Women*, New York: Oxford, 1999.

Kumar Ashok, *Women in Contemporary Indian Society*, New Delhi: Anmol Pub., 1993.

Kusum: "Can Wife be Made to Give Up Job? *The Hindustan Times*, Jan. 4,1976.

Lateef, Shahida: *Muslim Women in India, Political and Private*

Realities: 1890-1980s, New Delhi: Kali for Women, 1990.

Law, Bimla Churn: *Women in Buddhist Literature*, Ceylone: N.E. Bastian, 1927.

Lederer, Wolfgang: *The Fear of Women*, N.Y.: Arun and Strattan, 1968.

Mehta, Hansa: *Indian Woman*, New Delhi: Butala & Co., 1981.

Mehta, Rama: *Socio-legal Status of Women in India*, Delhi: Metropolitan Book Co., 1982.

Mehta, Raman Lal: *The Western Educated Hindu Woman*, N.Y.: Asia Pub. House, 1970.

Mehta, Raman Lal: *Thesis on the Legal Rights of Women under Different Communal Laws in Vogue in India* Bombay: The Advocate of Indian Press, 1933.

Mehta, Sushila: *Revolution and Status of Women in India*, Delhi: Metropolitan Book Co., 1982.

Menon, M. Indu: *Status of Muslim Women in India*, Delhi: Uppal Pub. House, 1981.

Meyer, Johann Jakob: *Sexual Life in Ancient India: A Study in the Comparative History of Indian Culture*, N.Y.: E.D. Dutton & Co., 1930.

Minault, Gail: *Secluded Scholars, Women's Education and Muslim Social Reform in Colonial India*, Delhi: Oxford Univ. Press, 1998.

Misra, Rekha: *Women in Mughal India*, Delhi: Munshiram Manoharlal, 1967.

Misra, R.N.: *Women Education and the Upanishadic System of Education*, Allahabad: Chugh Pub., 1993.

Mittal, Mukta (ed.): *Women in India, Today and Tomorrow*, New Delhi: Anmol Pub., 1995.

Moddie, A.D.: *The Brahamanical Culture and Modernity*, Lond.: Asia Pub. House, 1968.

Mohanty, Jagannath: *Education for All*, New Delhi: Deep and Deep Pub. 1994.

Moneil, Elton B. and Rubin Zick: *The Psychology of Being Human*, San Francisco, Canfield Press, 1977.

Montagu, Ashley: *The Natural Superiority of Women*, N.Y.: The Macmillan Co., 1968.

Mujtaba, Sayid, Lari, Rukni Musawi (Translated by Goulding, F.J.): *Western Civilisation Through Muslim Eyes*, Qum, Iran: Ansariyan Publication.

Nanda, B.R.: *Indian Women*, Delhi: Vikas Pub. House, 1976.

Pal, B.K.: *Problems and Concerns of Indian Women*, New Delhi: ABC Pub. House, 1989.

Pandey, Rekha: *Women from Subjection to Liberation* : New Delhi, Motilal Pub., 1989.

Pandit, S.K.: *Women in Society*, Delhi: Rajat Pub., 1998.

Paul, Diana Y: *Women in Buddhism*, California: Asian Humanities Press, 1979.

Phandis, Urmila: *Women of the World*, Delhi: Vikas Pub. House, 1978.

Pinkham, Mildreth Worth: *Women in the Sacred Scriptus of Hinduism*, N.Y.: AMS Press Inc., 1941.

Pujari, Premlata and Kaushik, Vijay Kumari: *Women Power in India*, Delhi: Kanishka Pub., 1994.

Rajgopal, T.S.: *Indian Ideal of Womanhood*, Calcutta: Ramakrishna Mission, 1969.

Ramabai, Saraswati Pundita: *The High Caste Hindu Woman*. Philadelphia: Jas. B. Rodgers Printing Co., 1888.

Ranganathan, Sarala: *Women and Social Order: A Profile of Major Indicators and Determinants*, New Delhi: Kanishka Publishers, 1998.

Rege, Y.M.: *Whither Women*, Bombay, The Popular Book Depot, 1938.

Rehman, M.M. and Biswal, Kamala Kanta: *Education, Work and Women: An Enquiry into Gender Bias*. New Delhi: Commonwealth Publishers, 1993.

Rohrbaugh, Joanna Bunker: *Women: Psychology's Puzzle*, N.Y.: Basic Books Inc., 1979.

Ross, Aileen D.: *The Hindu Family in its Urban Setting*, Toronto: Univ. of Toronto Press, 1961.

Sachidananda and Sinha, Ramesh P.: *Women's Right: Myth and Reality*, Jaipur, Printwell Pub., 1984.

Sengupta, Padmini: *The Story of Women of India*, New Delhi: Indian Book Co., 1974.

Sharma, Anuradha: *Women and Work, Human Resource Management Perspective*, New Delhi: Gyan Pub., 1999.

Sharma, S. Ram. (ed.): *Women's Education in Ancient and Muslim Period*, New Delhi: Discovery Pub. House, 1996.

Sharma, Usha and Sharma, B.M.: *Committees and Commissions on Women Education*, New Delhi: Commonwealth Pub., 1995.

Shridevi: *A Century of Indian Womanhood*, Mysore: Rao and Raghavan, 1965.

Sikri, Rehana: *Women in Islamic Culture and Society: A Study Family, Feminism and Franchise*, New Delhi: Kanishka Pub., 1999.

Singh, Indu Prakash: *Women, Law and Social Change in India*, New Delhi: Radiant Pub., 1989.

Singh, Uttam Kumar and Nayak, A.K.: *Women Education*, New Delhi: Commonwealth Pub. In association with Dr. Zakir Institute for Non Formal and Continuing Education, Discovery Pub. House, 1996.

Sinha, Anjana Maitra: *Women in Changing Society*, New Delhi: Ashish Pub. House, 1993.

Srinivasan, M.N.: *The Changing Position of Indian Women*, Delhi: Oxford Univ. Press, 1970.

Status of Women in India, A Synopsis of the Report, National Committee on the Status of Women (1971-74), New Delhi: The ICSSR, Allied Pub., 1975.

Subbamma, Malladi: *Women, Tradition and Culture*, Delhi: Sterling Pub., 1985.

Suguna, B: *Working Women and Religion*, New Delhi: Discovery Publishing House, 1994.

Tandon, R.K.: *Women, Nature, Education, Teaching and Rights*, Commonwealth Pub., 1996.

Thomas, P.: *Women and Marriage in India*, Lord: George Allen and Unwin, 1939.

Thomas, P.: *Epics, Myths and Legends of India*, Mumbai: D.B. Teraporevala, 1961.

Thomas, P.: *Indian Women Through the Ages*, N.Y.: Asia Pub. House, 1964.

Tikoo, Prithvi Nath: *Indian Women*, Delhi: B.R. Publishing Corporation, 1985.

Trivedi, Harshad R: *Scheduled Caste Women Studies in Exploitation, with Reference to Superstition, Ignorance and Poverty*, Delhi: Concept Pub. Co., 1976.

Upadhya, Bhagwat Saran: *Women in Rigveda*. Delhi: S. Chand and Co., 1983.

Usha, Rao N.J.: *Women in Developing Society*, Delhi: Ashish Pub. House, 1983.

Vashishta, B.K.: *Encyclopedia of Women in India*, New Delhi: Parveen Encyclopedia Pub., 1976.

Vreede de Stuers.: *Girl Students in Jaipur: A Study in Attitude towards Family Life, Marriage and Career*, N.Y.: Assen, Van Gorcum and Co., 1970.

Vyas, Anju and Singh Sunita: *Women's Studies in India*, New Delhi, Sage Pub., 1993.

Index